JUST THE

JUST THE JOB

Take Control of Your Career
For The Job You Want

John Best

NICHOLAS BREALEY
PUBLISHING
LONDON

First published in Great Britain by
Nicholas Brealey Publishing Limited in 1994
21 Bloomsbury Way
London WC1A 2TH

ISBN 1-85788-034-X

British Library Cataloguing in Publication Data
A catalogue record for this book is available from the British
Library.

Typeset by Servis Filmsetting Ltd, England

Printed and bound in Finland by Werner Söderström Oy

CONTENTS

ACKNOWLEDGEMENTS

I would like to thank the following for their help:

Hubert Hull, Managing Director of Bennington Training
Services.

Carly Stevens, Tutor, Open University and Norwich City
College.

Derek Chadwick, John Porteous and Steve Butler of the
Employment Service for their help in developing the
original idea.

All those who passed through our Job Search seminars in
Southern England over the past 2½ years who took the
trouble to complete our review forms and make helpful
suggestions. I only hope that we were able to help you and
that you are all back on the career path once more.

FOREWORD

I greatly admire the aims of John Best. As companies strive to adjust to the constantly changing and ever tougher competitive environment, more and more people go through the shock and trauma of redundancy.

In the overwhelming majority of cases this is neither a reflection on their abilities nor the result of any misfunction on their part. Being made redundant is a shattering blow to anyone's self-belief and can destroy the confidence which is so necessary if they are to rebuild their lives. Unless redundant people are offered help they all too easily become permanent casualties, resulting in their experience, resourcefulness and drive being wasted – something which the country can ill afford.

It is extraordinarily difficult to see redundancy as an opportunity rather than a threat, but this can be the starting point to actually rebuilding the future. I very much hope that John Best's book will help those who find themselves in this difficult situation.

Sir John Harvey-Jones MBE

PREFACE

This book was originally designed to help those executives, managers and professionals whose jobs were made redundant during the shake-out of the late 1980s and early 1990s.

The London and South-Eastern Region of the Employment Service gave a tremendous amount of help in supporting the development of the book and it is still used on Executive Job Search Seminars in that region and in parts of the South-West Region.

By April 1994 over 3000 executives will have used the original book and their comments and suggestions have helped to make this version more broadly based, more constructive and, perhaps most important of all, 'user friendly'.

For new readers, whether your concern is:

- career planning and management;
- finding work after redundancy;
- starting out on the executive ladder;
- returning after a career break;

you will find information, techniques and advice in this book designed to help you achieve success.

Good luck in your future career!

INTRODUCTION

Are you in control of your career? Do you know where you are going – or are you drifting along hoping something better will appear round the next bend? If you don't have a job at the moment, how do you go about getting a fresh start?

You may be looking for your first job, returning after a career break, facing up to redundancy, or just reassessing your position and prospects – in every case to be successful you need to have a clear idea of where you want to end up. Only if you know your destination can you plan your route.

The world of work has changed significantly in recent years and will continue to change. Previously you were considered to be showing your loyalty if you stayed with one employer throughout your career – now most employers are looking for people with experience, qualifications and a breadth of knowledge that is unlikely to have been gained from just one employer. As well as having several employers, it is also common for people to change direction during their career, even to quite a significant extent – a doctor becoming a hospital chief executive, an engineer becoming a counsellor, and so on. In addition, because of the way that organisations and work are now being structured there are fewer jobs and not as many of them are on a full-time basis.

If you are prepared to be flexible and to manage your career, then these kinds of changes can work in your favour. Nevertheless you have to be more determined than ever and more skilful at spotting opportunities and marketing yourself – because there are more people with better qualifications competing for fewer jobs.

Wherever you have reached in your career path you will

find something in this book to help you plan your next move. There is information on how to research prospective employers, tips on writing an effective CV and how to get your CV noticed, ways of preparing for interview and techniques for the interview itself, and strategies to ensure that you make the right contacts and use them to your advantage.

Which road you take will depend on your goal, and the kind of goal you have in mind will vary from person to person. Many people reading this book will insist that any work they undertake, any job they accept or any contract they agree to *must* be enjoyable – for them the financial rewards are less important than the content of the work and the job satisfaction.

Others, who have lost the ability to maintain their lifestyle through the recession of the late 1980s and early 1990s, have very hard decisions to make. A certain level of income is necessary to pay the mortgage, keep the car, pay for children's education or continue the social life they previously enjoyed. Their work ambitions will be governed to a significant extent by the salary on offer, and they may well feel obliged to compromise on the desire for job satisfaction in an attempt to maintain living standards. In addition, they may feel guilty or face recriminations if they are unable to meet the expectations of those who rely on them for financial support.

LAYING THE FOUNDATIONS

The reasons for seeking work are complex. The reasons for applying for specific jobs are even more complex and reflect the aspirations and circumstances of the individual job seeker. They can include:

- package offered and salary sought;
- level and areas of responsibility of job;
- job scope and content;
- prospects;
- location;
- organisation's ethos, product or reputation.

The above list is far from exhaustive and will vary greatly from person to person.

Let's try to find your starting point. Why are you looking for a job?

- I am unemployed, my previous job was made redundant, and I need an income.
- I have just left full-time education and want to get my foot on the first rung of the career ladder.
- I want to return to employment after a break of six years bringing up my little girl.
- My career has come to a halt in my present job and I need to look further afield to make progress.
- The project I am working on will end in six months' time.

Why do I want to work?	
What motivates me?	
Money	yes/no
Being creative	yes/no
Helping others	yes/no
Being occupied	yes/no
Managing others	yes/no
Job satisfaction	yes/no
Meeting other people	yes/no
When do I want to work?	
Only Monday to Friday	yes/no
Weekends	yes/no
9 am – 5 pm	yes/no
Evenings only	yes/no
Mornings only	yes/no
Any time	yes/no

Whatever your reasons for seeking a new job, you will find that it will require all your attention and a lot of hard work – *in fact finding the right job is a full-time job in itself.*

A JOB FOR LIFE?

As late as the early 1980s the concept of a job for life was still seen as a distinct possibility in many areas of employment. The public sector, for example, used to be a significant area of 'lifetime' employment, not only for manual staff but every grade including chief officers of local councils, public utilities and major civil service departments. Now even these bastions of promotion by length of service have been breached and limited contract appointments are common in all of them, together with regular performance reviews measured against imposed targets.

There has always been a misconception that the private sector was different: every employee lived on a knife edge and to survive required a year-on-year record of successful application and commitment. In fact, the private sector contained just as many safe havens and just as many examples of jobs where you brought dismissal on yourself only through sheer stupidity.

Dismissal or redundancy from a bank used to be unheard of (unless you had been foolish enough to put your hand in the till). Even poor customer care was only enough to have you moved off the counter. The same could be said of the major insurance companies, chain stores, and large industrial concerns. Job security in such areas as newspaper publishing or the docks was synonymous with lifetime employment.

Those days are gone – almost certainly for ever – and the successful job holder of the future will have to cope with a career encompassing frequent training and retraining, stringent annual performance assessments which have a direct effect on pay or promotion prospects, changes of location, changes of function – *and* changes of employer.

Productivity has become the watchword of the 1990s. Despite claims that productivity cannot be measured in some areas of employment – teachers, traffic wardens, police, the medical profession – there are nevertheless ways of combining effectiveness and performance to give a productive outcome. It is not a question, for example, of issuing more parking tickets but of deciding which areas are to be covered, whether traffic flow is improved and whether relations with the public are maintained at high levels.

A successful career in terms of continuity of employment and upward progression will need to be planned, flexible and continuously under review.

1
Starting Points

CAREER MANAGEMENT
REDUNDANCY
NEW TO THE WORKPLACE
MARKET RETURNERS

CAREER MANAGEMENT

Career management could well become a profession. There is already a profusion of agents in professional football, negotiating terms and conditions on behalf of their clients in much the same way as the acting profession has been organised for decades. Short though a professional footballer's playing life may be, agents often negotiate contracts for several years and then, when other potential employers enter the scene, renegotiate better terms and conditions with the existing club or a new one.

Some specialist recruitment agencies or headhunters would find very little difference in their *modus operandi* if they were to become career managers for a selection of well-qualified clients whose talents are likely to be in demand.

I once worked with a colleague in a financial institution. We were in our mid-twenties, recently qualified, with, we thought, good prospects for advancement. Fortunately we were not in competition with each other, as his sights were set firmly on a career with the current employer while he knew that my intentions lay outside.

After working late one evening, my colleague showed me his forecasts of his career path. On a very large sheet of paper he had described the current situation of all 268 staff in our particular specialism across the UK, South Africa and the West Indies. He had notes on their qualifications and likely promotions, linked to their retirement dates.

He had plotted the posts he should try for and those he should avoid in order to reach the post of departmental director by the age of 45–48, which traditionally would guarantee him a seat on the board before retirement.

Then came the proof that he had discarded me as a competitor. He asked me if I would lunch with him and his current girlfriend because: 'before I suggest we get engaged I would be grateful for your opinion of her as a hostess. As you can see I shall need a wife who can do a lot of entertaining.'

> I was lost for words – my career planning had never gone beyond the next potential move and my own job satisfaction.
>
> I gave him my opinion after the lunch and always like to think that I saved a very attractive and intelligent woman from a husband who saw her as a career development tool rather than a partner.
>
> The sequel is that our department was eventually closed but by the age of 42 my erstwhile colleague was deputy general manager of a major financial institution. I lost track of him after that but have no doubt that he achieved his aims.

Did my colleague 'go over the top'? Of course he did, but nevertheless there are lessons to be learnt.

How do you become your own 'career manager'? Short-term and medium-term objectives can only be attained by planning, by ensuring that you meet the relevant criteria. To achieve this you will need knowledge of the jobs market and how it is developing so that you are not caught in blind alleys.

You must be aware of the qualifications required and, most important of all, you must know how to sell yourself to potential employers and have the expertise and experience which will make you a desirable product.

Knowing how to research the business of an organisation you feel could offer you opportunities is vital if you are to make it clear how you meet that employer's needs. You will want to be able to convince the decision maker that an awful lot of time, trouble and expense can be saved by talking to you rather than entering the recruitment market. All these areas are covered in later chapters of this book.

Can you really claim that you can organise, manage and develop others if you can't organise, manage and develop yourself?

REDUNDANCY

Redundancy is a frightening word – particularly if it's your job that has been made redundant or you believe that it could happen.

If you need to continue to work but your job disappears, or you decide to make a move before job cuts are imposed, then you are a job seeker – in competition with many others.

Your starting point will be to make an inventory of what you have to offer a potential employer. Although you may have some advantages over the competition, you are still going to have to search very hard to find opportunities that you consider worthwhile.

Use the inventory on page 10 as a start. Points in your favour could include:

- a long and steady work record;
- good experience, skills or qualifications;
- excellent references from your present employer;
- a redundancy payment which means you can spend some time looking at the market rather than needing immediate earnings;
- a network of contacts;
- your employer may provide some help to start your job search.

Remember that redundancy is now a common situation for many managers and executives. There is life after redundancy, as many thousands have proved.

Despite the shock and despair that many people experience on being forced to search for a new job, you must realise that you can plan to overcome a lot of the problems you now face.

Identifying the problems and the ways in which they can be tackled is a vital first step to getting yourself back to work.

Inventory no. 1

What advantages do I have in my search for work?

1.

2.

3.

4.

5.

6.

7.

8.

9.

10.

Do I lack anything that I can put right easily?

1. Keyboard skills?

  Are there day or evening courses I could take to teach me how to use a computer?

2. Basic computer knowledge?

  Evening classes at the local school or college?

3. Interview techniques?

  Should I seek professional advice?

  Are there any courses offered by the Employment Service?

4. Anything else?

Your redundancy package

Current employment law is complex, so you might consider seeking free advice, perhaps from your trade union, ACAS or your staff association, to ensure that you know your employer's legal obligations. There are also many solicitors who have the expertise to help you, but this will cost you money.

 SEEK ADVICE

Do also take reliable financial advice regarding what to do about your pension – the options available are complex and a bad decision can have significant consequences on your income in retirement.

Some people in 'redundancy shock' neglect to push for the best possible package for themselves. Try to negotiate:

- retention of your company car for a period of time;
- favourable purchase terms for your company car;
- retention of other fringe benefits for a time, eg:
  - health insurance;
  - life and/or sickness insurance;
- pension entitlements and transfer values;
- outstanding holiday or bonus entitlements;
- help for your job search – typing, photocopying etc;
- help in setting yourself up in business – perhaps some contract work, recommending your services to others, or some space or secretarial assistance until you are on your feet, or even giving guarantees to potential clients;
- payment for outplacement or consultancy assistance.

All these benefits have been negotiated with companies or offered at some time.

Getting the right start

Points to establish with my present employer:

1.

2.

3.

4.

5.

6.

7.

8.

9.

10.

11.

12.

Your family

There is another main source of support which will be invaluable to you or – if you handle things badly – a major irritant and worry: your family.

Your immediate family, whether this is your partner, mother or father, should be a significant source of support – particularly as you all realise how your lives could change.

- Will the family lifestyle change? Will your family members accept the changes which may be necessary?
- Have you any dependants – can you still help them?
- Can immediate family members contribute more to the 'central fund'?
- What expenditure can you shed and what must be continued?

Hiding your problem from the family – hoping it will go away and they need never know – is a recipe for disaster. It will increase the trauma for them when they do find out!

You must bring the situation into the open and let them know what is happening as soon as you know. You must seek their support and make them feel part of the recovery exercise.

Your finances

Finance plays a major role in all our lives and you will need to come to terms with your loss of earnings as soon as possible.

List your outgoings and mark those which are essential:

- mortgage payments or rent;
- council tax, house and contents insurance;
- car loan, credit cards, other loans;
- living expenses.

The quick finance check on page 14 may help you to assess your position. Can you get help with any of this expenditure?

Go and see your creditors and tell them about your situation.

If you want to take stock of your financial situation in more depth, complete the family net worth form on page 15.

Quick finance check		
Essential expenditure	Monthly payments £	Amount outstanding £
Mortgage payments/rent		
Council tax		
House/contents insurance		
Personal insurances		
a.		
b.		
c.		
d.		
Current borrowings		
Car		
Furniture		
TV		
Credit cards		
Access		
Visa		
Others		
Family living expenses		
Other expenses		
a.		
b.		
c.		
d.		
TOTALS	£	£

Family net worth	
Assets	£
Cash	
Savings accounts	
Shares	
Home (market value)	
Other property (market value)	
Vehicle(s)	
Money owed to you	
Cash value of life insurance	
Jewellery	
Paintings	
Silver	
Household furniture	
Antiques	
Other assets	
Total assets	£
Liabilities	
Current bills due	
Money owed by you	
Taxes payable	
Mortgage, home	
Mortgage, other property	
Balance due, vehicles	
Balance due, hire purchase	
Other debts	
Total liabilities	£
Net worth = total assets – total liabilities =	**£**

Selling assets is a potential means of raising cash and it is helpful for you to decide which asset would be sold first if and when absolutely necessary, but with good planning on your part it may not come to that.

It may also be helpful to complete the monthly income and expenditure planners on a regular basis. Fill in the projected income or expenditure and then each month indicate the actual figure received or spent. Note the variance and use it to plan the next month. If expenditure is exceeding income, cut out all non-essential items.

Be careful not to duplicate expenditure, for example the individual elements of the job campaign costs (see below).

Estimated job campaign costs	
Computer	£
Computer supplies	
Ribbons/cartridges	
Paper	
Disks	
Software	
Stationery	
Subscriptions	
Reference books/manuals	
Copying expenses	
Telephone	
Answering machine	
Parking	
Petrol	
Other travel	
Postage	
Outside word processing	
Printing	
Subsistence	
Other	
Total estimated job search costs	£

Monthly income planner			
	Projection Month: £	Actual Month: £	Surplus or (Deficit) £
Salary			
Severance pay			
Holiday pay due			
Other company benefits			
Retirement income			
Unemployment benefits			
Interest from savings			
Dividends from shares			
Rental receipts			
Tax refund			
Interest from loans			
Interest from insurance			
Collection of debts			
Earnings – spouse			
Earnings – children			
Earnings – part-time			
Borrowing – life assurance			
Other			
Other			
Total income	£	£	£

	Monthly expenditure planner		
	Projection Month: £	Actual Month: £	Surplus (Deficit) £
Current bills due			
Hire purchase			
Interest on loans			
Mortgage payments			
Rent			
Gas			
Electricity			
Water			
Telephone			
House/contents insurance			
Council tax			
Car loan			
Car insurance			
Car maintenance			
Car tax			
Petrol/oil			
Life assurance			
Medical insurance			
Food			
Clothing			
Dry cleaning			
Child care			
Education			
Newspapers			
Professional fees			
Entertainment			
Travel			
Gifts			
Job campaign costs			
Other			
Total costs	£	£	£

Follow the advice below:

- Talk to your bank manager and building society manager.
- Make an appointment with the New Claims Adviser at your local Jobcentre and find out what benefits you are entitled to.
- If you receive a lump sum as part of your settlement – no matter how large or small – put the whole amount into a high interest account until you have had time to get advice on the best way of using it.
- Don't be tempted to pay off your mortgage at once.
- Don't rush to pay off the car loan.
- Read the small print on your loan agreements – you may find you have some insurance cover against unemployment.
- Make sure you get advice from several sources, not just one or even two – everyone wants to make sure you lodge your precious nest egg with *them*.
- Take as much time as you consider necessary to decide how you will use the money to gain the most benefit. Seek out experts who are reputable and who can advise you how to become tax efficient with maximum security.

DON'T TAKE
HASTY ACTION

Your opportunity

Redundancy is not something you have sought – it is traumatic for you and your family – but if it has happened the best way of facing it is to view it as a challenge and an opportunity.

How many times in the past have you wondered if your job, your way of life or your future were really what you wanted them to be? How often have you secretly wished for a change?

Now you have been forced into a situation of change you must take time to ensure that you make the most of it. It is probably the last opportunity you will have to change direction, to look at your future critically and to influence where you will be and what you will be doing for the rest of your life.

TAKE TIME

NEW TO THE WORKPLACE

If you are standing on the threshold of work for the first time, then view this as an opportunity to shape the rest of your life. Of course, you will have spent the last few years preparing for work and you will have your own ideas on what you want to do. You have probably had discussions with experts in career guidance and some potential employers, but suddenly it's down to you to make the crucial decisions.

When you are involved in making a very important decision within a very complex framework of circumstances, there are a few simple questions which may help you to shape your preferences:

- What would you like to do?
  Be practical – if you are 6 feet tall and weigh 12 stone you are unlikely to become a successful jockey.
- What do your skills, education or training enable you to do?
  Be realistic – a degree in computer science will take some explaining if you apply for posts in social work.
- Where do you want to work?
  While Cornwall is a lovely place to live, there is little call there for atomic physicists.
- Are you prepared to undertake training, periods of study or further education?
  Your A-levels or degree are only the entry ticket into a career – you will almost certainly need new skills.
- Will you compromise on starting salary to gain greater benefits later?
  This must be your decision, but in the present market many employers will expect you to contribute to your development.
- Is the decision to start work now the right one, or would you be better prepared by further full-time education?

What, where and with whom

What do I want to do?

What possible areas of employment have I considered?

What do my studies and examination results qualify me for?

Which geographic areas do I want to consider?

Which organisations offer career prospects which appeal to me?

What other factors will affect my choice of jobs?

Take a long, hard look at the area of work you want to enter:
- What are the normal entry levels?
- What are the qualifications and/or experience you will need?
- Can you succeed by being more formally qualified or by gaining both experience and professional qualifications while being employed?

Taking the time and trouble to analyse both your needs and the needs of employers in the area of work you wish to enter, and then trying to make sure that you match them, can pay rich rewards, not just to start with but as your career develops.

TAKE YOUR TIME

It is very easy, particularly at a time when jobs are hard to come by, to make a quick decision which you will later regret. Of course you can change tack – in fact you will be exceptional if you don't since the days of a job for life have gone. But you can make the development of your career much smoother and easier if you invest some thought and research time in making your decision.

The rest of your life will be influenced by the decision you make now, and that should be important enough to make sure you do not decide on impulse.

MARKET RETURNERS

Have you been away from the workplace for some time?

Whatever the reason – raising a family, a sabbatical, long-term illness, supporting a relative – you will find that the world has moved on and you have some catching up to do.

The approach to your return will very much depend on the area in which you have experience or want to work in now.

Let's look at a few examples:

- If you worked in electronics, in whatever sphere – communications, defence, safety, games, musical instruments, computer design – even a year away from the 'sharp end' will mean that you will be out of touch with developments. New improved chips, laser technology, optoelectronics, liquid sensors – there will have been advances in all technologies.
- What has happened in the defence industries since the Berlin wall came down?
- In accountancy, new software packages will have increased the speed at which work is done and provided greater opportunities to make models and projections in more detail, and with greater accuracy, than before.
- If you are a more generalised administrator or manager, can you cope with cost centre accounting, budget management or localised administration?
- What are the new 'buzz' words of your profession?

- What new developments are about to happen or have 'come on stream' recently?
- What is likely to happen in the financial services field with the increasing use of 'switch' cards and other plastic innovations? Will we all be organising our financial affairs by data link within a few years?

If you are to succeed in finding a way back to employment, it is essential that you get your research right!

- What will the employer's needs be?
- Can you meet those needs?
- Will you need retraining?
- Can you prepare yourself, by research and practice, to meet the current demands of your chosen profession?

Just putting yourself back into the market without research and preparation, without identifying potential employer needs and without self-assessment, is the road to nowhere.

Remember the old adage, 'F*ailure to prepare is preparing to fail*!' Time spent in getting yourself to the starting line fully aware of all the selling points you must put across will be time invested in your eventual success.

My executive search

As a returner to the job market:

What were my main areas of expertise?

Which areas of employment will these skills transfer to?

What jobs would I really like to do?

Consider your answers to the three questions above to decide what jobs you want, the areas of employment you are suited to and the expertise you can offer.

2
The Jobs Market

We have become accustomed to a frequently changing jobs market throughout the UK on a local, regional and national scale. The European Community operates a free market with increasing movement between separate states, and opportunities, events and trends will cross boundaries and affect our personal jobs market.

Some of the most important current influences are described below.

- *The peace dividend* Since the dissolution of the communist superpower based around the Soviet Union there has been a dramatic decrease in the demand for weapons, communications and defence systems.

  A very large slice of the gross national product of many Western countries – not least the UK – was previously spent on developing defence systems designed to keep ahead of the Eastern bloc (and of course vice versa).

  The swift decline in defence industries has particularly hit the south, south-east and Thames Valley areas of the UK, where for decades the development of electronic warfare and defence systems has provided a significant source of employment.

- *The housing industry* With rising unemployment all areas of the housing industry have faced recession.

  The decline in house sales has caused the closure or merger of estate agents. The financial services industry has suffered the results of the decline in house sales.

  A 50 per cent decline in activity in the construction industry has led to immense difficulties for architects, planners and surveyors together with construction and contracting staff. There has also been a parallel effect on furniture and white goods producers and retailers.

- *The advance of information technology* Many companies are replacing the 'friendly face' with the plastic card and the modem. Banks and building societies, insurance companies and other financial institutions have all made swingeing reductions in the number of people they employ, but claim to have maintained the level of service through the use of new technology.

Some banking services can be conducted entirely by telephone without any form of personal contact or use of 'high street' premises.

● *Increasing competition* Those industries which have been forced into competition from previous monopoly positions have in particular had to cut their workforces.

British Telecom is a prime example as it seeks to become a world leader in communications while facing increasing competition in the domestic market. The coal-mining industry now faces competition from imported coal and is seeking to reduce costs by shutting uneconomic pits. The privatisation of the ship-building industry has meant even further reductions in ship building in the UK.

While the examples given are mainly domestic, similar changes have been taking place across Europe which only serve to exacerbate the labour market over-supply in the UK.

The dramatic changes in Eastern Europe have led to the virtual closure of the now unsubsidised and therefore uneconomic industries of the former communist bloc, which has meant a devastating reduction in employment in those countries and led to pressure to reintroduce support and subsidies to offset the effect of free market competition.

All these developments, national and international, have brought about drastic changes in the jobs market. It is now almost entirely a buyer's market and for the last few years the only major growth industry has been unemployment.

This has taken many job seekers by surprise and caused them to take the view that there is little for them in terms of career development.

However, like every other market, the jobs market is constantly changing. Unemployment at 10 per cent means that 9 out of 10 people have a job. With 90 per cent employment there are a minimum of a million job vacancies every year, probably many more.

People still retire – are promoted – leave to raise a family – go abroad – change jobs. Some companies still expand – create new ideas – develop new products.

There are always employers seeking new workers.

YOUR PLACE IN THE MARKET

Every employer wants the best skills available – you are selling your skills for the best price you can achieve. You both want success and success will benefit you both.

Where are you in the jobs market?

Which sector of industry?
> Public, private or quango
> Administration, finance, manufacturing
> Production, research, development
> Engineering, retail, service
> Other

How has the recession affected your employer?
> Hit badly   Not at all
> Some downturn   We benefited

Is your job likely to survive?
> Things are getting better
> Status quo likely
> Changes could be on the way

Are you equipped to survive?
> Can your skills be used elsewhere in the company?
> Are you ready to seize other opportunities?
> Are there opportunities with other employers?
> Will your skills/qualifications become out of date?
> Have you planned to update/upgrade your skills?

Are you planning ahead?

Are you managing your future?

So here you are in the marketplace – a marketplace which changes, if not hourly at least daily – and you need to make a sale to survive. You are the product – what must you do to ensure a sale?

Rule no. 1 – Before you can sell anything you must first research your market.

All potential employers, when contemplating recruitment, need candidates with specific skills, knowledge, experience, physical capabilities or the ability to be trained.

- What have you got to sell?
- What price can you put on the skills or experience the employer needs or you can offer?
- Is there a meeting point between the two?

Reaching that meeting point involves letting the employer know you are there, that you have the abilities required, that your needs are met by the employer's offer and that you can be of benefit to each other. How can you get there?

   Normally you will know about the employer but they do not know about you.

Rule no. 2 – No one can buy a product unless they know it exists!

You are the sales person – *you* must take the initiative. Your sales strategy will be based on:

- product knowledge – identifying what you have to offer;
- job opportunities – identifying your potential customers;
- your curriculum vitae – preparing your sales brochure;
- the interview – closing the sale.

There are two stages:

- your CV, on which you depend to secure and lay the framework for an interview;
- the interview itself, during which you must build on the favourable impression you have already created.

A positive outcome will follow if:

- you inspire confidence that you meet the employer's needs, and
- it is clear to both sides that the job meets your needs.

You must, if you really want to succeed, do the ground work, carry out your research and get your preparation right.

There are many others competing for the same 'customer' and only one can make the 'sale'.

SELL YOURSELF

Now get down to some executive decisions

Where is your marketplace?
> Local to your home
> Within a set geographical area
> UK only – if yes, where
> Europe only – if yes, where

Define your job market
> Which sector

Sales	Accountancy
Management	Other
Engineering	

> Level of responsibility
> Salary range
> Future prospects
> Small company – large company – public sector – private sector

What does a job have to offer to attract you?

High salary	Solving problems
Reward for effort	Achieving
Helping others	Other
Being the boss	

Other considerations

3

Discovering Yourself

SKILLS ANALYSIS

PUTTING THE PIECES TOGETHER

Before you can write your CV – your sales brochure – you will have to:

● carry out a thorough analysis of your skills, knowledge and experience;
● look at yourself from a recruiter's viewpoint so that you can present the information required in an attractive and interesting way.

SKILLS ANALYSIS

As well as assisting with the preparation of your CV, your skills analysis provides you with a foundation to review the direction of your job search and change direction if it is appropriate.

A clear understanding of what the recruiter needs to know will enable you to select features as benefits against defined needs.

To begin your skills analysis use the prompt list on this page and the next to identify those activities which have enabled you to develop your skills. Think of examples drawn from your present or past employment or from your studies to show your skills, aptitudes, knowledge and experience. Remember to include activities which have taken place outside your employment.

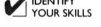

IDENTIFY
YOUR SKILLS

Prompt list
People
Working with others
Supervising/managing others
Establishing internal or external contacts
Communicating – writing
– explaining
– persuading
– negotiating
Appraising
Training/coaching/counselling

Technical

Problems	– analysing/defining
	– originating/devising solutions
	– implementing decisions
Organising	– establishing loadings and resources needed to meet demands
	– setting priorities
	– allocating resources
	– devising systems
	– monitoring quality/quantity
Information	– eliciting
	– handling
	– defining
	– producing
	– working with computers
Controlling	– budgets/targets/schedules
	– establishing and monitoring performance
Production	– improving systems/methods to increase output
	– preparing estimates
	– eliminating delays

Personal

Taking risks/speculating
Originating/creating
Taking responsibility
Meeting deadlines
Coping with emergencies
Working under pressure

Complete inventory no. 2. Having established the skills and experience you have to offer – the vital assets in your job search – you hold the key to your future.

Inventory no. 2

Make an inventory of all the assets you have which go to make up your sales brochure.

Make a list of the **knowledge** you have: *I know*
what makes a computer work
how to make final accounts interesting

What **skills** do you have that an employer may need? *I can*
design effective advertisements
negotiate complex leases

Describe below the details of your experience and qualifications.

Experience: *I have*
prepared full company accounts to trial balance stage
managed the equipping and commissioning of a new hospital in Saudi Arabia

Qualifications: *I have gained*
NVQ level III in Sales and Marketing
Membership of the British Institute of Management

Now you can identify and research those areas of the jobs
market which offer you the greatest opportunities for a full
and rewarding career and in which your main assets can be
put to best use.
   For example:

Accounting technician
    + sales experience
        + computerised accounts training
            = sales office accounts manager

Management experience
    + fitness
        + budgeting
            + like working with people
                = sport or leisure management

The executive jigsaw

Where do you fit?

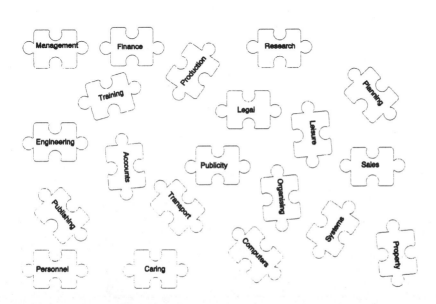

4

Finding the Jobs

ADVERTISED VACANCIES

CONTACTS

NETWORKING

DIRECT APPROACHES

WHICH WAY FOR YOU?

Once you have identified the skills and experience you have to offer, you can start searching out potential employers who may have vacancies that attract you.

Unless the opportunities you find meet your needs and ambitions and require some, or all, of the skills and experience you possess, then they are probably best left alone. You might feel that there are some vacancies for which you could apply with a proviso that you will need training before you can be fully effective. You should note this very carefully in any approach you decide to make.

So where are you likely to find employment opportunities?

ADVERTISED VACANCIES

The first, and most obvious, area to search is among the vacancies which are advertised! This includes:

- national press advertisements;
- local press advertisements;
- professional journals;
- television – CEEFAX and ORACLE.

National press advertising is the usual way in which an organisation indicates that there are opportunities for employment available.

The choice of newspaper – *Daily Telegraph*, *The Times*, *Sunday Times*, *Guardian* – will depend on the areas in which the newspaper specialises or is seen to specialise by job seekers. For example, a great many secretarial vacancies are carried in *Today*, vacancies in the building and construction industries in the *Daily Express* and educational vacancies in the *Guardian*. The *Daily Mail* offers a free helpline giving access to an individually tailored selection of the previous six weeks' vacancies.

The main areas currently covered by the major newspapers on each day are shown below.

Newspaper	Monday	Tuesday	Wednesday	Thursday	Friday
Daily Telegraph	Most disciplines	Most disciplines		Major supplement covering most disciplines	
Guardian	Creative – media and marketing	Educational International	Social services Health Finance Personnel Youth work	Computing Science and technology General management Finance and business	Housing – Conservation Town planning Leisure
The Times	Educational Newspapers Office	Legal – solicitors Public sector Health care Public finance Multilingual vacancies	La crème de la crème (secretarial) Media Marketing	Executive opportunities	Information Technology
Daily Mirror		Major appointments day			
Today		Secretarial Catering Some others		Full supplement Engineering General	
Daily Express		General appointments	Career Plus feature	Career Plus feature	
Daily Star				Jobs Extra Engineering Security Construction Clerical Sales	
The Independent	Engineering Computerlink Science and technology	Accountancy Financial and City	Media Creative and marketing Sales	Education and tuition Graduate opportunities Public Medical Legal General	General appointments Financial Legal
The Mail				Career Mail Management and executive Engineering and technical Sales and retail Secretarial	

Remember, the Sunday papers carry large numbers of recruitment advertisements at all levels.

Local newspapers are an excellent source of vacancies – most local companies, local authorities and public service vacancies are always carried locally as well as nationally.

The local daily (mainly evening) papers have special days for recruitment advertising – often Thursday – but carry some advertisements every day. Some weeklies, particularly the county-wide papers, also carry recruitment advertising, often at senior level.

It may be necessary for you to order the paper for a neighbouring town to ensure that you do not miss opportunities which are within travelling distance. For example, in the north-west the *Manchester Evening News* and the *Liverpool Daily Post* serve contiguous areas and both would be relevant in either area.

Make a list of the newspapers you should be reading:

Morning:

Evening:

Magazines:

Don't forget that many of these will be available at your local library, since it can be expensive to buy them all each week.

CONTACTS

Although you may not yet have identified them, you will have contacts who may know of jobs becoming vacant.

Start by making a list of all the contacts you have and then think how they may be able to help. Don't try to think of people who might actually offer you a job – that list would be very short!

Who are *your* contacts? When you have identified your contacts, how can you optimise the help they may be able to offer you?

 DON'T ASK
FOR WORK

People who are asked for work automatically clam up. People who are asked for help and advice often respond positively. Everyone likes to be able to help but hates being asked to do something when the answer must be 'no' – so word your request with great care.

Do they have their own contacts that could give help or advice, perhaps people of influence in the careers field? Always seek their agreement before you use their name.

 FOLLOW UP

If you do contact someone they have referred you to, make sure you go back to your original contact in a positive vein. 'I followed up that lead you gave me and I'm seeing Mr Jones next Tuesday' could well lead to: 'Great, I hope something comes from it. Let me know what happens.' This keeps you in the person's mind and other leads could follow.

People who can help me

Personal contacts

Name and address: Tel:

Name and address: Tel:

Name and address: Tel:

Name and address: Tel:

Name and address: Tel:

Business contacts

Name and address: Tel:

Name and address: Tel:

Name and address: Tel:

Name and address: Tel:

Name and address: Tel:

Suggested contact letters following referrals
Dear Mr Jones

Keith Smith, a close friend of mine, has suggested that I contact you as someone who may be able to advise me about my future career. He felt that your knowledge of the current climate would enable you to comment on my aspirations.

Following a reorganisation of the structure of my present employers, XYZ Bank, I am leaving after some 15 years. My CV is attached so that you can see my progress to date.

I should be most grateful for any comments or advice you feel able to give. If I may I will telephone you in a week's time to see if you can spare some time to see me.

Yours sincerely

*   *   *   *

Dear Mr Greene

I recently met John Miles, a senior executive at XYZ Bank, who suggested that I contact you for advice and guidance on my future within the financial services area.

John thought that you might know the key people whom I should contact for guidance in developing my role in the specialist field I hope to work in.

My CV is enclosed to enable you to see my career progress to date. I will contact your secretary next week in the hope that you may be able to spare some time to discuss my future.

Yours sincerely

Lest I forget!

Keep a note of the contact letters you send and the dates for follow up.

Letters sent to: Follow-up date:

NETWORKING

Networking will be a vital aspect of your job search.

There are a whole range of organisations which can offer you help in different ways:

- Your local reference library will have directories covering all the local companies and what they do.
- Employment and recruitment agencies will know the local labour market and can give you guidance.
- Your adviser at the Jobcentre will have sources of employment information which are regularly updated.
- The planning department of your local council will have information on planning permissions granted to companies moving to the area or expanding their present premises.

Make a list of the organisations you should keep in touch with.

DIRECT APPROACHES

Part of your plan to get back to work must be forming your own contacts by a direct mail approach.

This simply means contacting companies you have identified which need the skills and experience you have to offer and which might therefore be interested in you – when they know you exist! Even if they do not have an opening at the moment, they may keep your details on file for opportunities which could arise in the future.

Making speculative contacts can pay off in a variety of ways. Even if you have no luck with a particular employer you may be referred or recommended to another who is interested. Use any meetings you get to gain more information about the job market. Each employer you see is a new contact. Each rejection you experience is one step nearer the job you want.

I know a man who can

My network of contacts and support

Address and tel. no.   **Contact name**

Government departments:

Recruitment agencies:

Voluntary and other organisations:

So how do you go about finding organisations to approach? You have made summaries of your skills, experience and abilities. You have identified relevant areas of employment. Now you can start linking these assets to potential employers.

- A good starting point is your local reference library. A sample of the directories you might find useful is shown on page 47. Get used to finding your way around these directories – they are full of helpful information.
- Read the business pages of your local newspaper – go to their office and look at the back numbers. They may also allow you to see archive files on specific companies which will detail everything that has been reported.
- Don't miss the local radio or television news and business programmes – they are packed with information on businesses in your area.
- Talk to your Jobcentre adviser about the local business scene. Ask which companies are recruiting, not necessarily in your field – all recruitment indicates an upswing.

Keep records of all the information you collect – you may want to refer to it two or three weeks later.

Approaching organisations direct

Follow the sales approach to a prospect, which is:

- locate the decision maker;
- send a mailshot to create interest;
- make it clear that you will be following up your approach.

How do you identify the decision maker? Is it the personnel manager or the chief executive? The objective should be to identify the person who has the problem – often the line manager to whom you would report if you joined the company.

Using trade directories

British Companies Index – provides extracts of annual reports, profit records, share price movements.

British Middle Market Directory – lists medium-sized companies showing location, activities, sales turnover, when founded and directors.

Guide to Key British Enterprises – financial data on turnover and capital, details of trade, trade names, trading styles, list of directors by name and function, assessment of company size and range of activities.

Regional Directories of British Industry and Services – company information region by region.

Stock Exchange Year Book – provides a brief financial description of all quoted public companies.

Times 1000 Leading Companies – background information on all major firms including products, growth and number of employees.

UK Kompass Register – published annually in two volumes: one gives basic facts on company location, activities, staffing; the other is an index of products and services cross-referenced to supplying companies.

Who Owns Whom – gives details of relationships between companies: subsidiary companies, main board companies and locations and brief information on performance.

The Municipal Year Book – gives comprehensive details on all organisations in the public sector, including all local authorities and so-called quangos (quasi-autonomous non-governmental organisations).

Extel Cards – information sheets on quoted and unquoted companies giving details of financial performance.

Register of Companies – latest accounts, balance sheets, names of directors and other financial information can be obtained from the Registrar of Companies, either in Cardiff (0222 388588) or London (071–253 9393).

There can be no set pattern for identifying the decision maker, but after some attempts you will find that you can circumvent the obstacles in your path.

> Robert, an ex-Staff Sergeant from the Royal Signals, saw an advertisement for a post as Manager of a Local Authority emergency service for elderly people living alone. The advert gave some details of the computer-based system for monitoring calls received via 'panic buttons' worn by the elderly on a chain round the neck.
>
> Before he put his CV together, Robert decided to telephone to try to get some information on the system so that any specifically relevant information could be highlighted. He spoke to the telephone operator who put him through to the appropriate department.
>
> He spoke to the current manager who invited him to call in to see the system. Robert went there that day and was given a guided tour and the information that the system was going to be reviewed within 12 months. The current manager was being promoted and would be influential in deciding on his successor.
>
> Robert was able to submit a very relevant CV, emphasising his experience in communications systems in relation to the two alternatives which were being considered for the future. Together with the fact that he had impressed his potential boss in their discussions, this put his appointment beyond doubt.

There are many other ways. A simple visit to the company and a chat to the receptionist will often give you all the information you need. It is very much easier for the person you contact to refuse over the telephone than face to face.

If all else fails a little deception is permissible:

● I would like to write to the manager of the XYZ department about an order we may place with your company. Could you give me his name and initials please?

● My daughter is completing a project on local industry.
  Could you tell me the name of the person she should
  write to for specific advice on your production methods?

Pete is a furniture salesman, specialising in selling to a
large number of retail outlets across a wide geographic
area. He had been unemployed for 18 months before he
attended a Jobsearch seminar.

Although he had been selling all his adult life he had
never before looked at himself as 'the product'. The
idea of 'selling himself on the open market' provided all
sorts of new possibilities for him.

He now drove an old van instead of his company car
and was very short of money, so when he heard of a
major furniture show being held 200 miles away it took a
great deal of ingenuity to devise a way of getting there
and appearing smart and businesslike.

Pete drove to the show overnight, arriving at around 3
am. He stayed at the nearest service station until 7 am,
sleeping in the back of the van, and then washed,
shaved and changed into his best (and only) suit.

He arrived at the show as it opened and started his
tour of the stands, looking for familiar companies to talk
to and, most of all, familiar faces.

It was hard work, but after three hours the reward
came. An old acquaintance offered him coffee and while
they were chatting asked Pete if he had heard that
another salesman they both knew was taking early
retirement following illness.

Closing the conversation as politely as possible, Pete
found his way to the relevant stand. Within the hour he
was being interviewed by the company's sales manager
who was at the show.

Two weeks later he was being introduced to his new
customers and his new company car was being delivered.

It took a lot of effort and self-belief to get to that
exhibition, but Pete is now an advocate of self-
marketing and knows that without it he could well still
have been out of work.

Your mailshot

How do you put together a mailshot which will create interest? The golden rules are:

- Keep it short – no more than three brief paragraphs.
- Type it – easy to read, easily assimilated.
- Paragraph 1 – indicates that your experience is relevant to the target's business.
- Paragraph 2 – your reason for writing.
- Paragraph 3 – the promise to follow up.

 ARGUE YOUR CASE

Give a specific reason for your contacting them – have a 'peg' on which to hang your letter. You are not 'asking for a job' or 'hoping they might have a vacancy'; you are making a business proposition, showing how your abilities can contribute to the success of their organisation. You must prepare a thoroughly argued case to prove that the cost of employing you is more than outweighed by the benefits that will result. Show how you would improve, develop or help the organisation to become more effective – and be sure you can deliver the goods!

No one ever got a job merely by writing a letter. Aim for a face-to-face meeting and state this intention clearly when you write. Be prepared to fit in with the times the employer is available, and prepare for the meeting as you would for a job interview.

Suggested direct approach letter

Dear Mr Stokes

I read with interest the press comment concerning your move and expansion. As this may create new opportunities for people with my experience and qualifications, I am forwarding my CV for your consideration.

May I highlight the following areas which I believe are relevant:

- Extensive experience of office procedures, particularly related to computer systems and office technology.
- Specialised O&M experience.
- Organising and implementing clerical staff training.
- TQM and BS 5750 procedures.

I feel sure that I could make a substantial contribution to the continuing success of your company and will telephone you early next week to ask if I might call to see you.

Yours sincerely

Putting words in your mouth – your mailshot follow up

Remember – you must be yourself but promote interest.

1. Your contact with the switchboard operator or secretary:

   'May I speak to . . . . . please. This is . . . . . and he/she is expecting my call.'

2. Your first words to the contact:

   'Good morning/afternoon Mr/Ms . . ., this is . . . . You may remember I wrote to you last week concerning the possibility of working for your company because I believe I have experience and skills which would be attractive to your organisation.

   'May I take a few minutes of your time to discuss any opportunities that may be open now or in the future?'

3. Where you go from there depends on the next response. *Your* objective is to gain agreement for you to visit the company.

It is vital that you have a prepared script and that you have rehearsed it. Never start cold or you will flounder.

REHEARSE

Now prepare your own script for follow-up calls.

When you meet the potential employer you may have to make the running – after all, you asked for the meeting. Be business-like and professional in making your proposals:

- Ask questions about the employer's needs.
- Treat them as a client – tell them what you can do and what you offer.
- Be flexible and prepared to negotiate. If a full-time appointment is not feasible, they may be interested in employing you on a short-term basis for a specific project.
- Get any agreements – proposals or contracts – in writing as soon as possible.

✗ DON'T GIVE UP

If you really want to work there, don't take no for an answer. Occasionally persistence will pay off and after an initial refusal you will be offered a meeting. Make the most of it.

WHICH WAY FOR YOU?

Let's recap on the four main avenues back to work:

- advertised vacancies;
- your own contacts;
- contacts through networking and agencies;
- direct approaches.

Which are likely to be most productive for *you*?

The table on the next page gives statistics taken from a Bennington Training Services Job Search Workshop and details successes achieved by each method over a 12-month period. It might help you to formulate your plan and spend your time in the most useful way.

Age	under 30	31–40	41–50	51–60	over 60
Advertised jobs	4	8	10	6	0
Agencies/networks	5	6	5	3	0
Personal contacts	2	5	15	18	3
Direct approaches	1	8	25	30	1
Totals	12	27	55	57	4

Work out where you stand in the table and decide which of the avenues we have discussed is going to give you the greatest chance of success.

5

Your Sales Brochure

You are now well along the road to forming the basis of your sales campaign. You have:

- identified the product (you);
- listed your main selling points;
- researched the market for potential customers.

Now you have to let them know what a great product you have to offer them. What facts will help you to shape your sales brochure?

- What are the potential employer's needs:
  - skills;
  - qualifications;
  - experience?
- What can you offer to meet those needs?
- What have you achieved?
- What were the key activities of your last job?
- Could some training make you a better candidate?

FEATURES, BENEFITS AND ACHIEVEMENTS

The presentation of your CV is vital – it should be attractive and easily read. It must also be honest in all its claims. It should contain your features and benefits – the features that make you the most attractive candidate because they relate to benefits you can bring to your employer.

BE HONEST

Feature: I have travelled abroad extensively.
Benefit: My knowledge of other countries and their languages helps considerably in export sales.

The benefits you can bring are much more important to the potential employer than your features.

Hey! This is me

What features would you want to demonstrate to an employer?

1.

2.

3.

4.

5.

6.

7.

8.

What benefits could you claim to bring to an organisation?

1.

2.

3.

4.

5.

6.

7.

8.

The final section of your sales brochure will consist of a record of your achievements.

What have you achieved in your working life that is worth telling the world about?

Employers like to know about people who have:

- saved time or money with good ideas;
- improved how things are done;
- found ways of attracting customers;
- improved teamwork and spirit;
- suggested new uses for old products;
- used a computer system;
- reduced stock holdings;
- found ways to cut costs;
- increased profits;
- increased margins.

Your achievements do not have to be technical or massive. Simple ideas are often the greatest savers of time and money: improvements in filing systems; better ways of moving materials around; improving reception areas; getting goods to and from work sites; satisfying customers; getting information to prospective customers.

Everyone can identify something they have achieved, something that has helped 'oil the wheels' or improved the service on offer to customers.

However, while you must ensure that your achievements appear in your sales brochure, you must always be cautious at interview that you do not project yourself as knowing all the answers before you even know the scope of the job. Everyone fears a 'new broom' who is going to start sweeping away the present, comfortable situation.

What I have achieved

Within my working experience:

1.

2.

3.

4.

5.

6.

Outside the work environment:

1.

2.

3.

4.

5.

6.

CURRICULUM VITAE – THE STORY OF LIFE

Now that you have completed your self-assessment and identified your main selling points, you can start putting together your sales brochure – your curriculum vitae – for printing.

In the current jobs market it is not unusual for an advertisement to attract several hundred applicants. It is vital that your CV attracts attention and is therefore read if you are to have a chance of making it to the short list of, say, 10 people who will be invited for interview.

A golden rule is to target your CV individually to each separate vacancy that you apply for.

Hard work and time consuming? Certainly – but well worth the effort if it gets you to interview.

Although this is more difficult with speculative approaches – which must still be a part of your action plan – nevertheless if your research is done properly then there will be parts of your 'standard' or 'core' CV that you can change so that it becomes evident that you have a valid reason for the approach.

You will have about 40 seconds of the recruiter's time to gain attention!!

Attracting attention for the wrong reasons is easy, but it is much more difficult when you want to create a favourable impression.

Don't:

DON'T

- make amendments on a previously prepared CV;
- write your CV by hand, unless requested to do so – typewritten text is three times less difficult to assimilate than handwritten;
- use poor quality paper or envelopes;
- use coloured paper;

- fold your CV to get it into a small envelope;
- squeeze up information to save another page;
- put a CV through your present employer's franking machine to save postage;
- include certificates, references or examples of past work, unless requested;
- omit your age – it will often be assumed that you are hiding something if you leave it off.

 Do:

- put the facts briefly and clearly;
- use two pages if necessary – but no more!
- leave something to develop at interview;
- put the relevant information in the CV, not in the covering letter;
- ensure sufficient postage on the envelope.

If you are completing an application form:

Don't:

- say 'see attached CV' – the form has been designed to show information in the order the employer wants.

Do:

- take a photocopy before starting to complete the form.

How many times have you got half way through completing an application form in blue ink only to find the words 'please complete in black biro'?

Your CV is designed for one purpose – to get you in front of the decision maker at an interview.

You must therefore be prepared to spend a considerable amount of time and effort making the document as effective as possible for each and every job you apply for.

The research you do on the post, the way you relate your experience, skills and knowledge to each post, the amendments you make to your core CV to attract the selector's eye, your ability to ensure that the CV reflects your confidence that you can do the job – all these will contribute to success or failure.

Remember, failure to prepare is preparing to fail.

What does the recruiter want?

Have you really read the advertisement you are responding
to? Have you examined the information sent to you with
the application form, analysed it and made notes?

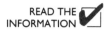

READ THE
INFORMATION

   Have you sat back and thought about the situation,
putting yourself in the position of the recruiter for this job
and writing down what you want from applicants?

A finance-based company advertised for sales
representatives saying they wanted 'lateral thinkers'
for new development work. The advert ended with the
words: 'please attach a recent photograph to your CV'.
   Out of some 200 replies:

- 12 per cent had omitted photographs and were
  instantly discarded.
- 82 per cent had enclosed photographs of
  themselves and were considered for interview.
- 6 per cent – 12 people – enclosed recent
  photographs of all sorts of topics, including the
  mother-in-law, my dog, a big toe and Lands End in
  the dark.

All those falling into the last group were invited to
interview and eight of them were appointed. They
had considered the advert in depth, linked up the
request for a recent photograph with the requirement
for lateral thinking, and cracked the coded message.

Not many recruiters go to such lengths, but there are often
messages in advertisement or job descriptions which you
ignore at your peril.

COMPILING YOUR CV

Now is the time to start putting together your core CV – your database for all future job applications.

There are five main sections to the successful CV:

1. Relevant personal details.
2. Brief details of your education with examination results.
3. Precise details of vocational training, particularly mentioning professional qualifications.
4. Employment record – *in reverse chronological order*, the latest employment being shown first. This should be structured to highlight the last 10 years – only show brief details for employment before that.
5. Other *relevant* information – this should include any achievements not related to previous employment, eg an award for charity work, certificate of advanced driving, played for county rugby XV, hold a pilot's licence.

As has been said elsewhere, what is left out is as important as what goes into a CV.

At this stage it is as well not to mention that you will need three weeks off every year with pay to attend your territorial army summer camp – or to say that you are heavily committed to the local council and need to attend three meetings each month.

You do not want to raise doubts. Unlike *This is your life*, your CV should not contain anything that can be used to surprise you at an interview. For example:

- CV: I am Secretary of the Liberal Democratic Party in Peckham.
- Interviewer: Mrs X, did you know that this company has contributed to the Conservative Party for years? In view of your political views, wouldn't you find this embarrassing?

or:

- CV: I left company X because I did not agree with their policy of exporting goods to South Africa.

● Interviewer: Mr Y, are you aware that we have branches
  in South Africa and have had a presence there since
  1906?

Similarly, you must bear in mind that the person compiling
the short list is human. He or she may well have all sorts of
biases, likes and dislikes, preferences and turn-offs. So
keep away from those things which could be controversial
or could imply to someone who does not know you that you
hold extreme views or actions, have lots of time committed
to something other than your job, or have an evangelistic
attitude which would transcend your work.

DON'T BE
CONTROVERSIAL

   In short, you need to make your employment record and
achievements, you education and/or training and your
interest in the organisation stand out in your application.
   What will make a potential employer stop at your CV and
examine it more closely?
   Your last job will be a key area of interest to the person
reading the CV. You should provide them with the clues
they are seeking and provide yourself with the opportunity
to promote your suitability.
   Try the exercise on page 64 to help you define the
purpose and objectives of your most recent job. Be certain
of the meaning of the words you use.
   You need to define this information so that the reader of
your CV is able to understand the full scope, objectives
and responsibilities of that post.
   After you have carried out this exercise several times and
are happy with the result, ensure that you keep notes of all
the relevant information so that you can easily refer to it
when necessary and adapt the format to suit a variety of
applications.

KEEP NOTES

Your most recent job

What was the job title?

What did that title mean within the organisation?

Would it mean the same to another employer?

What were the main purposes of the job?

List the key objectives:

List and quantify your main responsibilities:

Below is an example of the finished product:

Job title: Divisional Accountant

Responsible for a team of 10 staff producing management and financial accounts.

Key objectives: 1. To help the management team increase profits on turnover.
                   2. To maximise return on capital employed.

Key activities: 1. To devise and maintain appropriate management information systems.
                   2. To ensure that information is presented in clear and usable formats.

On page 66 you will find a simple chart which will help you devise an effective CV database. Complete it carefully, in pencil to start with, or, like an application form, take some photocopies for practice. When you are satisfied with the final format, ensure that you make several copies – having done all the hard work you don't want to lose it.

After you have established all the core information in an easy-to-use format you will be able to put together a CV which will be relevant to any post for which you are suitable and will contain all the information under the five headings on two pages of A4.

If that sounds a tough assignment, just think of the poor person at the receiving end of the exercise faced with reading perhaps 200 CVs. Which would you select to examine in detail – the concise, well-presented CV, or the 10 pages which seem to have no end and no beginning?

Thinking of that person now could help you later – so make the format of your CV attractive, easy on the eye, use lots of white space and make the relevant information stand out clearly.

Information recruiters will need

EMPLOYMENT (include company name, industry, product/ service, size)						
RESPONSIBILITIES for people (ie number and level): operations: finance:						
WHAT DID I DO? people: operations: finance:						
AUTHORITY TO MAKE DECISIONS concerning people: operations: finance:						
ACHIEVEMENTS relating to people: operations: finance:						
WHAT DID I ENJOY MOST AND LEAST?						
EDUCATION AND TRAINING						

You should present information in the following format:

CAREER HISTORY	
Name:	George Sprago
Address:	1 Wherego Drive
	WETHAM
	Oxon
	OP1 2NS Tel: 0400 200000
Date of birth:	8.10.46 Married

There will be occasions when you want to bring information from the 'other information' section into the first part. For example, if the post requires you to drive, it would be worth adding possession of a clean driving licence to this section.

Part 2 of the CV concerns your education, and could be set out as follows:

Secondary education:	GCE/CSE/GCSE examination results
	eg 6 O-levels and 3 A-levels
19XX–19XX	OND/HND/Degree
	Show subjects and grades as appropriate

Details of subsequent professional and vocational training, examinations passed and qualifications achieved should be shown in a similar format and make up part 3 of the CV.

Training undertaken on your own initiative and more formally based training should receive equal prominence. Be sure to include all *relevant* training – do not underrate anything you have achieved.

Differentiate between specific training – eg driving a forklift truck – and more general training – eg supervisory skills.

Part 4 of your CV describes your work history and provides the opportunity for you to explain how your career has progressed to date. The idea of progression is attractive to most employers – a simple list of jobs done will not provide the linking which is necessary to show how you have grown and developed. Five jobs in ten years might give the impression of a 'flitter' who cannot stick at anything; whereas a single company over the same period could be interpreted as applying to a 'stick-in-the-mud' with little drive or ambition.

You have to show the route you have taken and make it seem logical and attractive – the result of planned development allied to opportunity.

George Sprago's career history, detailed on page 69, was compiled in application for the job of Production Manager at a corrugated carton manufacturer. It shows how he made the best of his employment history:

- The current/last job and its relevance to the opportunity now on offer are shown.
- The job title without related responsibilities would mean very little. Similarly, the relationship between the responsibilities and duties is clearly shown and easily identified at first glance by the person making the selection.
- The main achievements are set out to attract attention but still leave plenty of scope for discussion at interview on how they were brought about.
- The remainder of the employment section shows how the move to Horncastle came about, the areas of experience which preceded it and how Sprago's career within Horncastle has progressed over a 12-year period.

CAREER HISTORY

PERSONAL DETAILS

Name: George Sprago

Address: I Wherego Drive
WETHAM
Oxon
OPI 2NS   Tel: 0400 200000

Date of birth: 8.10.46   Married

EDUCATION AND TRAINING

1957–1961   Secondary Modern education
1962–1969   Seven-year apprenticeship – Letterpress Machine Manager

EMPLOYMENT

1977–date   Horncastle Packaging
Printers – packaging and cartons

Works Supervisor   1989–date
Responsible to Production Director for a team of 40: overseers, printers, warehouse staff and unskilled staff engaged in printing, cutting and creasing, hot foil blocking and gluing cartons.

Duties include:
Staff – recruit, train, set objectives, appraise and discipline staff under my control.
Customer contact – receive orders from Sales Office, plan production, liaise with clients.
Control – through overseers control work carried out in composing room, print room and finishing departments.
Negotiate – with subcontractors for work put out, ensuring quality standards are maintained and within agreed prices.
Health and safety – ensure that regulations are observed.

ACHIEVEMENTS
● Improved quality – won Jubilee Award in 1985.
● Achieved a stable workforce by setting clear objectives, ensuring that craftsmen could work unhindered, improved productivity by 20%.

Working Print Room Overseer   1986–1989
Responsible to Works Manager for 15 printers engaged in cartons, labels and packaging.

Machine Manager   1977–1986
Responsible to Print Room Overseers for letterpress, printing, cutting and creasing and hot foil blocking.

1975–1977   Bundsworth
General Printers
Machine Manager – Letterpress

1961–1975   Porter and Stout
Printers
Apprentice – Letterpress Printing

Finally in your CV you should include any other relevant information. This will very much depend on the post you are applying for. Examples which could all be relevant in the right circumstances include:

- I speak fluent Spanish – olé!
- I have an extensive knowledge of Chinese food.
- I am a very successful amateur photographer.

Your research will indicate the information you should include.

GETTING YOUR CV NOTICED

The purpose of the CV is to get you to the interview stage. Your objectives therefore are:

- to get the CV noticed – and read;
- to ensure that it matches the recruiter's needs so that you will be among those receiving a positive response.

Some potential candidates use various 'tricks of the trade' to make that initial impact.

For example, it is a proven fact, from research carried out among recruiters, that a photograph on the top right-hand corner of a CV, *not* obscured by a covering letter, will attract the recruiter's eye. Quite often this leads to a more interested look at the content of the CV – which is exactly what you want.

Of course this is an individual decision. Perhaps you are afraid that a current photograph will indicate that you are older than the stated age range, or you feel that photographs do not do you justice. Only you can make the decision.

What about starting with a 'capsule profile' to attract attention?

- Janet Walenski is a self-motivating personal performer with excellent people skills and a high level of commitment.

- Jack Smithers is an innovative self-starter with a track record of team motivation and success-related achievements.

These are examples of actual profiles received – only the names have been changed to protect the authors! But what do they mean in terms of an employer's needs?

Obviously no one is going to write a profile that says:

- Tom Mix is an idle individual although well qualified. He prefers to earn the highest possible salary for the least effort.

So if you do want to write a profile it must be short and simple and address the employer's needs directly. For example:

- Jackson Buchanan has an honours degree in electronics, state-of-the-art experience in fibre optic communications and is currently working in LCD control systems.

Simple, direct and to the point – no 'buzz' words.

KEY WORDS

So-called 'buzz' words can hold considerable dangers in CV writing:

- Will the reader interpret them as you intend?
- Are they still in use or will they appear outdated?
- Are they widely used or peculiar to your company?

There are, however, groups of words which we all use that have defined meanings in the recruitment field. You must ensure that if you use them you are fully aware of the interpretation which will be put on them. For example:

Decisive	Able to make decisions, judgements and take action
Stress tolerance	Maintains performance in pressure situations

Judgement	Makes decisions based on logical assumptions which reflect factual information.

On page 73 you will find more examples of words and phrases frequently used in the recruitment process by both candidates and recruiters. The list is not exhaustive and you may wish to add to it to describe your skills and achievements. However, you will find it helpful in defining your own management skills and in constructing your CV.

These key words come and go in various sectors of the employment field. Keeping your own dictionary can be a useful source of reference.

GETTING THE INTERVIEW

Take time over preparing your CV:

- Make sure your CV does you credit – that it puts your case forward in the most structured way in relation to the job you seek.
- Make sure all your claims – examinations, skills, qualifications, past jobs and areas and levels of responsibility – can be substantiated at the interview or later.
- Make sure your CV arrives on time – even if you have to deliver it by hand – and that it is attractively presented.

Your CV is you!

- **You on paper.**
- **Your working life story.**

It represents your only chance of getting an interview.

One of the main objectives of this book is to get you in front of potential employers – to be interviewed for jobs!!

Your CV is the vehicle for achieving this objective for yourself after completing the other parts of your job search plan. You owe it to yourself to spend time and trouble getting the CV right.

It is your sales brochure – make sure you include all the *benefits* you will bring to the employer you have selected.

GET YOUR
CV RIGHT

Key words

Qualities
Adaptability	Maintains effectiveness in changing environment
Compliance	Conforms to organisational policies
Flexibility	Can modify approach and style to gain objectives
Independence	Confidence in your own convictions
Integrity	Honest, trustworthy and reliable
Risk taking	Calculates benefits gained against possible loss
Tenacity	Sticking to a problem until a solution is reached

Interpersonal skills
Communication	Ability to express oneself clearly either orally or on paper
Listener	Can receive and react to oral information
Persuasiveness	Gains support for own policies or viewpoint
Sensitivity	Conscious of problems and needs of others
Sociability	Can mix with others in an effective and participative manner
Teamwork	Supportive of others/contributes to team goals

People and organisational skills
Delegation	Effective control of subordinates and resources
Development	Maximising skills and competence of self and subordinates
Environmental perception	Aware of effects of changing economic/social factors
Leadership	Can lead others/a team in an effective and supportive manner in achieving corporate ends
Organisational awareness	Perceives corporate effect of decisions or activities
Organisational design	Ability to determine effective corporate structures
Planning/ organisation	Establishing effective plans to achieve objectives

Decision-making skills
Creativity	Develop innovative and imaginative solutions to perceived problems
Entrepreneurial ability	See opportunities to increase profitability, develop new business avenues or adapt to new opportunities
Numerical analysis	Understand, organise and present numerical data
Problem analysis	Identifying problems and, through thorough research and data analysis, isolating causes
Vision	Focus on major goals as opposed to individual issues and see the whole picture as the major objective

Motivational skills
Commitment	Belief in own ability and role as valuable to the organisation and putting company interest in advance of self-interest
Energy	Capacity to work hard, maintain drive and direct a high level of activity
Initiative	Actively influencing events, seeking opportunities and originating activity
Personal motivation	Need to obtain satisfaction and achieve demonstrable success
Resilience	Able to maintain effectiveness despite adverse situations, disappointments and rejection of ideas!
Work standards	Setting and achieving standards for self and subordinates

The covering letter

People often ask how they can make the covering letter attractive and attention grabbing.

On a scale of 1 to 10 the importance of the covering letter is 0 when responding to advertised vacancies! It is virtually impossible to influence the recruiter about your suitability for the job on offer *before* he or she has read your CV.

If that seems to be a dismissal of what you may have considered to be a very important document – and it remains important for mail shots or speculative approaches, as discussed before – then think for a moment about the poor recruiter faced with over a hundred CVs from which to compile an interview short list.

He or she has a list, either on paper or a mental list, of the basic requirements needed to qualify for an interview and a remit to select, probably, twice the number needed for interview to give to the person who will do the final selection.

Having put all the CVs in piles, the natural procedure is to turn over the covering letter and look at the CV to identify those which meet the qualities on that list, for example:

- has led a research team;
- has degree/HND in electronic engineering or computer science;
- has experience of both digital and analogue links to optoelectronic communications systems.

Only if these priorities are met do two things happen:

- the remainder of the CV is read to establish other plus or minus points;
- the covering letter is read.

Because of this, a covering letter for an advertised job can be as simple as:

Dear Sir

Appointment of communications research team leader

Having read your advertisement in the I.E.E. News dated 4 December 1993, I enclose my CV for your consideration.

I should be delighted to supply any additional information you may require.

I look forward to hearing from you shortly.

Yours sincerely

PREPARING FOR A RESPONSE

You have taken a great deal of time and effort to put together an attractive and informative CV – in order to get yourself invited to an interview.

It is vital that you take as much trouble to ensure that an unexpected approach does not kill off your chance before it has even had time to evolve.

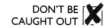
DON'T BE CAUGHT OUT

How is the telephone answered in your home?

Very often a recruiter will decide to make an informal call to clarify a particular item on your CV or settle a niggling doubt. Also when the interviews are to take place at short notice the invitation to attend can come by phone.

Are you prepared? Or will a possible employer hear something like this:

> Ullo! What? . . . yeah, this is 123456 . . . What? . . .
> yeah, he's here, who wants him? . . . OK, I'll see if he
> wants to speak to you . . . 'old on, you're not one of
> those flaming double glazing firms, are you?

Anyone can make a mess of an unexpected phone call – *you* mustn't be caught unawares.

Practice makes perfect. You should rehearse your responses to a possible telephone approach and see it as an opportunity to find out information you need and to sell yourself as the number one candidate.

The best response to a telephone call is to give your number – then the caller has to take the initiative. Make sure the whole family knows that you could be receiving a call which could have a profound effect on all their lives.

> 666333 . . . Who's calling? . . . Yes, I'll call her to the
> phone.

Keep your response polite, brief and helpful.

6

The Interview

PREPARATION

AT THE INTERVIEW

Dear Mrs Edwards

Appointment of Sales Administrator

I am pleased to invite you to attend a selection interview for this post on Thursday 1 August.

The interview will take place at our Administrative Centre in Edison Street and you should arrive at reception at 10.50 am.

Will you please confirm that you will be attending.

Yours sincerely

Personnel Manager

So you've made it to interview – congratulations! Now the really hard work starts to make the most of this opportunity.

PREPARATION

What do you know about the company?

- What does it do?
- How many people work there?
- Is it well known locally?
- Have there been any recent news stories about the company:
  - have they won a large order;
  - have they laid off staff or had a strike;
  - are they making a profit?
- What skills are required by the people who work there?
- Do they sell to the retail market or specialised users?
- Do you know what their products/services are?
- Are they part of a larger group of companies?

The questions are endless – but you need the answers!

How *are* you going to get the information you need to ensure that you don't get caught out at the interview?

- Do you know anyone who works there?
- Your local newspaper will have back numbers of the business pages. Go and look at the last few months' editions.
- Telephone the company and ask them to send you a copy of their latest annual report.
- Take a walk past the premises – this can be very revealing.

Completing the information checklist on page 80 will help you approach the interview with greater confidence and you will find the time spent worthwhile. Photocopy the checklist and complete a fresh one for each interview.

Completing this checklist will provide you with interesting and relevant information which you can use to answer some of the more common questions used by interviewers.

Why are you interested in this post?

- This job interests me because I successfully covered most of the areas of responsibility in my last job.
- You seem to be looking for someone who could grow with the company and accept more responsibility as the workload increases.
- The job offers an appropriate level of responsibility and the rewards seem to match the challenge you are offering.
- I saw in the local paper that you are seeking planning permission to extend your distribution warehouse. While you are currently looking for someone with my experience in distribution control, in future that person will need the flexibility to manage expansion during a developing and often chaotic new building programme. I have been through that very successfully before.

And this is them!

Organisation name:

Interview address:

Interviewer:

Head office address:

Other branches/units:

What the company does:

Number of people employed   – locally:
                                   – nationally:

Is it a PLC?

Last year's results: – profit £
                                   – loss £
                                   – turnover £

Recent publicity/news reports:

Your assessment of its future prospects:

Any other information/comments:

The needs of the job (eg accountancy skills):

How you will fit in the team (eg flexible, adaptable):

Your needs (eg level of responsibility):

Take some time to look at the questions on the next few pages and identify answers using the information you have collected. Fill in your main answers on the checklist on page 85.

For example, how would you respond to the question: 'We all have weaker areas – how would you describe your weaknesses?' Perhaps your answer could be along the lines of:

● I cannot bear going home and leaving unfinished business.

In response to a question about relationships with others, you might say:

● Of course there are people who are difficult to get on with – but I would never let them know that I felt that. Most people respond to courteous and considerate treatment.

Most questions can be turned to your advantage. Preparation is the key – prepare and go to your interview with confidence.

Even if the information you gain about the organisation is limited, for whatever reason, you can still plan to elicit what you do not know at the interview and turn it to your use. For example:

● How long has the company been operating?
● Is this a new post? How did the vacancy arise?
● Are there any special problems associated with the job?
● Who will I be working for?
● Who will I be working with?
● Do you expect to offer training for the successful applicant?

You must be selective and react to the answers you receive – but practise your response to alternative situations.

BE PREPARED

Questions you could be asked at interview

- What do you know about us as an organisation?
- What do you think we are in business for?
- How did you learn of this appointment?
- What do you think you can do for us?
- Tell us about your last job/present job.
- Give a brief summary of your career to date.
- How did you get your last post?
- What would an average day comprise in your last job?
- What have you enjoyed doing during your career?
- What has given you least pleasure?
- What were your main achievements in your last job?
- Did you experience any major career setbacks?
- Did you make changes which affected the success of your section/company?
- How do you think your last boss would describe you?
- Give some examples of the main problems you encountered and how you tackled them.
- How has your last post prepared you for greater responsibility?
- What in your previous job is relevant to the post you have applied for?
- How would you describe your last employer as an organisation?
- What advantages would there be to you if we offer you this post?
- How would you contribute to our success?
- Do you see the recession affecting us and if so how?
- How does this job relate to your career aspirations?
- In general terms how do you see the main developments in your field of work?
- Have you any other interviews in the near future?
- Why did you go to college/university?
- What made you choose the subject you studied?

- What other activities did you pursue at college/university?
- Did you take part in any voluntary activities?
- Did you hold any 'offices'?
- Have you had any unusual holidays?
- How do you think college/university/the forces contributed to your development?
- Have you undertaken any study or training since leaving college/university?
- Why did you not go on to college/university?
- How did you achieve your professional qualifications?
- Do you have any plans for further study?
- What do you consider to be your main qualities?
- What are your main weaknesses?
- What do you consider to be the most important qualities for a manager?
- What are your longer-term aspirations?
- How would you describe your health?
- Have you suffered any major accidents/illnesses?
- Would you change anything in your career so far if you had an opportunity to do so?
- What are the main factors you require in a potential employer?
- Where do you see yourself in five years' time?
- What was missing from your last job that you see in this post?
- What are your salary requirements?
- Are you seeking additional benefits?
- What are your main leisure pursuits?
- Have you any community-related responsibilities?
- Are you a member of any professional, social or civic organisations?
- Do you hold office in any of these?
- Do you have responsibilities which could impinge on your work such as reserve forces, magistrate or similar?
- Are there likely to be any reasons for unexpected absence requirements?

- How can we consider you with your lack of recent experience in this field?
- Why do you think you did not make more progress with your last employer?
- Don't you think you may be too old/too young for this post?
- Don't you feel you are a bit too specialised for us?
- Why have you changed jobs so frequently?
- Why did you stay so long with your last employer?
- Why were you selected for redundancy?
- What have you been doing during the time you have been unemployed?
- Would you be applying now if you had not been made redundant?
- Do you have any current problems we should be aware of?
- Have you never been married?
- Was your divorce in any way influenced by work problems?
- Is there anything else we should know about you?
- Are there any further questions you wish to ask us?
- How does this interview compare with others you have attended?

Checklist

Before each interview consider the following questions:

Why does this job interest me? Why did I apply for it?

Is there anything special about this job?

Is the level of responsibility right for me?

At what level will I be reporting?

What are the rewards?
Salary – bonuses – car – expenses – health insurance – pension – mortgage or removal expenses

Is this the type of organisation that will develop my career?

Will this job look good on my CV five years from now?

What will be the next step forward?

Is this an exciting opportunity?

Before the interview make sure you know:

- How do I get there?
- How long will it take to get there?
- How far is the office from the station/bus stop?
- Is there parking space nearby?

Complete a practice run on a working day.

Decide what you are going to wear and make sure those clothes are clean and pressed and your shoes are clean. Put on the outfit and make sure there are no missing buttons or broken zips – and make sure alternatives are available just in case a zip sticks on the day!

Do you have the telephone number of a taxi company in case the car doesn't start or the bus is full? Is there an umbrella handy in case of storms?

The rule is to take every possible precaution against last-minute upsets that will cause stress.

Also make sure that you have rehearsed your answers to the questions which are most likely to be put to you. Look again at the list of questions above and your prepared answers.

At a recent three-day seminar, Gordon came in on the second day to say he had received a telephone call the previous evening inviting him to an interview on the following day.

He had been called to seven interviews in the preceding year without success and admitted that on each occasion he had gone along fairly 'cold', without much research on the potential employers.

As a practical exercise the rest of the delegates drew up a plan of campaign to help Gordon be as well prepared as possible. Fortunately the seminar was being held in the town centre so resources were close at hand. Dividing up the tasks, the delegates spent the rest of the morning at the local reference library, the local paper's head office and on the telephone, and Gordon went to reconnoitre the company itself.

The results showed the following:

- This was a subsidiary of a major pharmaceutical company supplying international markets.
- The sales job Gordon had applied for could cover as many as 20 brand names marketed by the local company.
- Nationally the company employed 11,400 people at seven separate sites and the local site was also the distribution centre for central southern England and for Europe.
- The company had applied for planning permission to expand its local premises, but there were several objectors.
- The previous year's profits had been £8.6 million on a turnover of £3.2 billion, an increase of 6 per cent over the previous year.
- The company was involved in promising research on relief of arthritis.
- The local company worked a full day shift and both dawn and twilight short shifts.
- Gordon found that parking was at a premium and he would be better off using a public car park some 600 yards away.

Gordon went to the interview able to relate his skills and experience to the company and capable of holding a sensible discussion about this potential employer.

On this occasion he lost out after the third interview, but has since obtained a similar post.

AT THE INTERVIEW

When called in by the interviewer remember the following tips:

- Wait to be invited to sit down.
- Smile to show you are at ease.
- Look at each questioner and show you understand.

- Let them finish their questions before starting your reply – *never* interrupt.
- Don't smoke – even if invited to do so – but show you do not mind your interviewers smoking if they want to.
- Never swear, however mildly.
- Don't argue – use phrases like: 'yes, but perhaps' or 'on the other hand'.
- Never apologise for your own situation – being unemployed; your age; your children; your lack of paper qualifications.
- Do ask for clarification if you don't understand anything.
- Always be honest – you will be found out in false claims.
- Leave questions of salary, holidays, health insurance, company car etc until you are negotiating an offer.
- Respond to any invitation to ask questions:
  - clarify the 'company needs' for this post;
  - seek further information on anything which was not clear;
  - ask about the company's training policy;
  - what are the job prospects;
  - is the organisation likely to grow.
- Ensure that you have all the information you need to make a decision should they decide to make you an offer.
- Try to end by reaffirming your interest in the post *and the company*.

Every interview will be unique, in as much as every interviewer has a different style. However, all recruiters are looking for the same thing – to be reassured that the person sitting in front of them is the ideal candidate to fill the vacancy. Then their job is easy – they can make the recommendation that an offer is made and the post is filled.

To reach that conclusion they will ask questions and also invite you to ask questions. Typical questions which interviewers ask have been given in the previous section, and you should practise answers to all that could be applied to you.

However, there are three key questions which will crop up in every interview and, although the wording may differ slightly, the essence will be the same:

● Can you tell us something about yourself?
● What do you know about us?
● Is there anything you would like to ask me?

Can you tell us something about yourself?

Being invited to talk about yourself is the great sales opportunity.

The questioner does not want to know about your place of birth, your education, your first ever job or your favourite football team. He or she wants you to start selling yourself into the job.

What do you say?

> Thank you. When I saw the advertisement for a staff writer on your magazine I was really excited because in addition to my reporting experience, which as you can see from my CV is very extensive, I have a life-long interest in steam railways and have done voluntary work on the Watercress line.
>
> I think I am right in saying that you are looking for someone who can produce original work rather than just editing pieces sent in. Is that how you see it?

In a short time you have done two things – established your credentials for the job and taken the opportunity to clarify a point that you need to be sure of. You can then go on to talk, very briefly, about other aspects of *relevant* experience.

Address the interviewer's needs. What are they? How can you meet them? Close with a question, to keep control and elicit more information:

● Is that the way you see it?
● Am I right in assuming that this is what you are seeking in the right candidate?

- The experience I have outlined seems vital to the post on offer, don't you agree?

What do you know about us?

This question gives you the chance to show you have done your homework.

> Because of my interest in railways I have been aware of your magazine for some time and have read most of the recent editions. You have certainly established a niche in a growing marketplace and I understand your circulation has risen by 400 per cent over the last two years.
>
> I have been very interested in the way you have adapted to the changing nature of the supporters of steam railways and its movement from being perceived as a pastime for eccentrics to becoming a credible part of the leisure industry.
>
> You seem to have overcome the potential pitfall of becoming stuck on a plateau of interest to steam buffs only and started to reach the much wider leisure market. In fact, some of your articles have been quoted in TV documentaries on steam railways.
>
> I understand you are in a healthy financial situation compared to some of your competitors.

Is there anything you would like to ask me?

You are sitting there just bursting to ask questions:

- What is the salary?
- How long are the holidays?
- Can I have time off to go to my Council meetings?
- What sort of office will I have?
- What car is on offer?

Don't – leave all these questions until the post is offered.

Instead, try to 'close the sale' – what points do you want to get over that you haven't been able to make? You need to ensure that you have convinced the interviewer of your suitability for the job. Invite any objections at this stage when you have a chance to make a response.

> I understand your concern regarding the technical knowledge required to maintain standards with new technology and your move to on-line printing. Some of this will be new to me but I hope I have been able to convince you that I can handle those aspects. Are you happy about my abilities in that direction?

Do you want to re-emphasise anything? Do you need to clarify any points?

> You said there would be a lot of editorial freedom – who would clear any points of controversy?
>
> You implied you see this as a 'hands-on' job with a lot of the work being done on site. The bulk of my experience has been away from the desk and I would welcome the opportunity to operate in that way.

The three key questions

Can you tell me something about yourself?

What do you know about us?

Is there anything you would like to ask me?

7

Psychometric Tests

Psychometric tests of greater or lesser credibility have been around for almost a century: the first commercial tests were available as long ago as 1904. They were used extensively in the Services during the First World War and subsequently during the recession of the 1920s and 1930s.

Forms of tests were used to segregate school children during the inter-war years and for some time after the Second World War. The '11+' contained a filtering 'intelligence' test followed by more academically based examinations.

Following the virtual abolition of educational selection in state schools and the dramatic reduction in competition for jobs during the 1950s and 1960s, this kind of assessment fell into disuse. It was only when the business cycle returned to recession and larger pools of job seekers became common that employers decided that they needed further aids to selection.

WHAT ARE PSYCHOMETRIC TESTS?

The British Psychological Society defines psychometric tests as: 'instruments for the quantitative assessment of some psychological attribute of an individual.' They are used to distinguish between individuals on a number of attributes, most of which are not easily quantified in a verbal interview:

- *General intellectual ability* is measured to try to establish intelligence levels *per se*.
- *Aptitudes* – specific abilities – show the propensity to learn more readily in a given area and ability to apply intelligence.
- *Interests* can demonstrate additional abilities and the way in which an individual *wants* to progress.
- *Personality* attempts to quantify areas such as conscientiousness, sociability and anxiety, all of which can influence performance in certain occupations or in teams.

● *Personal qualities* are often measured by separate, more
  specific assessments. The Leadership Opinion
  Questionnaire is an example of a test designed to
  assess a person's position on dimensions describing
  their supervisory style.

TESTS IN THE SELECTION PROCESS

There are literally dozens of tests (variously called
assessments, methodologies or papers) available to those
who feel they need another dimension in the selection
process.

The main point to be aware of is that there is nothing to
fear from a properly conducted, reliable psychometric
assessment. It is far from being the crucial element in a
selection process but is part of a logical progression from
CV to interview to assessment.

Your CV is the first or nominal decision influencer. You
will never get a job on the basis of your CV alone, but it
allows the decision maker to decide whether you should be
seen. The next step, the interview, is known as the ordinal
stage.

However, how can the recruiter be sure that impressions
gained over a comparatively short time are accurate
enough to make the decision to appoint the 'number one'
candidate? Now the employer may wish to use a further
level of selection – the interval level.

The interval level is intended to measure by how much
various candidates differ, enabling the recruiter to make
judgements on fine differences of aptitude, attitude and
reaction to defined circumstances.

Although tests are most often used to refine judgements
already made in reducing a large number of candidates to a
final short list, some organisations, particularly in the fields
of financial services or sales, use assessments as an initial
filter to ensure that time is not wasted in interviewing
people who are totally unsuited to a sales or marketing
role.

It is perhaps the 'up-front' use of assessment, in a fairly basic form, that has given rise to the myth that psychometric assessment is a *test*, an examination, that must be *passed* in order to obtain employment. This has also given credence to the idea that the person being assessed can 'beat the system' by giving the answers that the organisation wants to see rather than answering truthfully.

Properly designed and applied tests cannot be manipulated and will not be used to filter out applicants. The great majority of assessments are made for genuinely useful reasons and are properly and fairly interpreted.

 DON'T BE AFRAID

As a candidate you should have nothing at all to fear from a psychometric assessment. Quite often it can be welcomed as a further opportunity to demonstrate your suitability for a job – provided you are applying for posts for which your skills, qualifications and experience suit you.

PERSONAL APPROACH QUESTIONNAIRE

The following questionnaire is a typical example of a format which analyses your personal approach to work. You might like to draw your own profile by answering the questions.

To gain a good understanding you must *not* try to cheat. Just work through from start to finish with a time limit of, say, 15 minutes *before* you even look at the scoring analysis.

When you have finished ask someone else, a friend or partner, to complete and total the score sheet.

It is a good idea to photocopy the questionnaire, or use pencil, so that you can have a second attempt *if you need to rethink your approach.*

Remember, there are no right or wrong answers – just a profile of you as you are.

If you want to know what you are saying about yourself in this test, consider the picture which the answers to each section would provide for a recruiter. You can then draw conclusions about your suitability for the post you are seeking.

Instructions

The Personal Approach Questionnaire helps you to describe your major and minor approaches to work with a view to identifying the positive and negative ways in which you use your strengths.

There are a number of self-descriptive statements, each of which is followed by four possible endings. You should indicate the order in which you feel each ending applies to you. In the blank spaces to the right of each ending fill in the numbers 4, 3, 2 and 1 according to which ending is *most like you* (4) and *least like you* (1).

Do not use 4, 3, 2 or 1 more than once for each statement. Even if the statements have two or more endings which seem equally like you (or unlike you), please rank them 4, 3, 2 and 1.

There are no right or wrong answers - the only correct answer is what you decide yourself.

Questionnaire

Section 1

I FEEL MORE PLEASED WITH MYSELF WHEN I:

A. act idealistically and with optimism ( )
B. see an opportunity for leadership and go after it ( )
C. look after my own interests and let others look after theirs ( )
D. adjust myself to fit in with the group I am with ( )

I AM MOST APT TO TREAT OTHERS IN:

E. a respectful and polite way ( )
F. an active and self-confident way ( )
G. a careful and reserved way ( )
H. a social and friendly way ( )

I MAKE OTHERS FEEL:

I.   well regarded, capable and worthy of being
     called on   (   )
J.   interested and enthusiastic about joining me
     in what I want to do   (   )
K.   justly treated, respected and appreciative of
     the consideration I give them   (   )
L.   pleased, impressed and desirous of having me
     around   (   )

IN A DISAGREEMENT WITH SOMEONE I CAN GAIN MORE
BY:

a.   relying on the other person's sense of justice (   )
b.   trying to outwit or outmanoeuvre the other
     person   (   )
c.   remaining composed, logical and immovable   (   )
d.   being open minded and adaptable to the other
     person   (   )

IN RELATING TO OTHERS I MAY:

e.   become confidential and give my trust even
     to those who do not seem to seek it   (   )
f.   become aggressive and take advantage of them,
     before realising I have not given them much
     consideration   (   )
g.   become suspicious and aloof and treat them
     with too much reserve   (   )
h.   become too friendly and find myself with
     people, even when I am not especially invited   (   )

I IMPRESS OTHERS AS:

i.   a naïve person who has little self-confidence or
     initiative   (   )
j.   a 'sharp operator' who always tries to get the
     best of the bargain   (   )
k.   a stubborn individual who is cold towards others (   )
l.   an inconsistent person who never takes a stand
     on my own   (   )

Section 2

I FEEL I CAN BEST WIN PEOPLE OVER BY BEING:

A.   modest and idealistic   (   )
B.   persuasive and winning   (   )
C.   patient and practical   (   )
D.   entertaining and lively   (   )

IN RELATING TO OTHERS I AM MOST APT TO BE:

E.   trusting, confiding and supportive of others (   )
F.   quick to develop useful ideas and organise
     others to carry them out   (   )
G.   practical, logical and careful to know who I am
     dealing with   (   )
H.   curious to know all about them and anxious to
     fit in with what they expect of me   (   )

I FIND IT MOST SATISFYING WHEN OTHERS SEE ME AS:

I.   a loyal and trusting friend   (   )
J.   a person who can take ideas and make them
     work   (   )
K.   a person who is practical and thinks for myself (   )
L.   a noteworthy and significant person   (   )

IF I DON'T GET WHAT I WANT FROM A PERSON I TEND TO:

a.   give up readily and justify the other person's
      inability to do it   (   )
b.   claim my rights and try to talk the other person
      into doing it anyway   (   )
c.   feel indifferent and find another way to get
      what I want   (   )
d.   laugh it off and be flexible about the whole thing (   )

IN THE FACE OF FAILURE I FEEL IT IS BEST TO:

e.   turn to others and count on them to help me out (   )
f.   fight for my rights and take what I really deserve (   )
g.   hold on tight to what I already have and keep a
      close eye on others   (   )
h.   keep up a front and try to sell myself as well as
      possible   (   )

I'M FEARFUL THAT AT TIMES I MAY IMPRESS OTHERS AS
BEING:

i.   submissive and impressionable   (   )
j.   aggressive and conceited   (   )
k.   cold and stubborn   (   )
l.   superficial and attention seeking   (   )

Section 3

I FEEL THE BEST WAY TO GET AHEAD IN THE WORLD IS
TO:

A.   be a worthy person and count on those in
      authority to recognise that worth   (   )
B.   work to establish a right to advancement and
      then claim it   (   )
C.   preserve and build on what I already have   (   )
D.   develop a winning personality that will attract
      the notice of others   (   )

IN SOLVING THE PROBLEM OF WORKING WITH A
DIFFICULT PERSON I:

E. find out from others how they have met the
    problem and follow their advice   (   )
F. match wits with and get around the other person
    as best I can   (   )
G. decide for myself what is right and then stand
    by my own convictions   (   )
H. change myself to fit in and make the relationship
    more harmonious   (   )

I IMPRESS OTHERS AS:

I. a trusting person who appreciates advice and
    counsel   (   )
J. a self-confident person who takes the initiative
    in getting people going   (   )
K. a steadfast person who deals with others in a
    conservative manner   (   )
L. an enthusiastic person who can fit in with almost
    anyone   (   )

I FEEL THAT IN THE FINAL ANALYSIS IT IS BETTER TO:

a. simply accept defeat and look for what I want
    elsewhere   (   )
b. engage in a contest of wits rather than lose out
    and get nothing   (   )
c. be suspicious and possessive, rather than give
    up what I have   (   )
d. compromise and go along for the time being   (   )

AT TIMES I AM APT TO BE:

e.   easily influenced and without confidence   (   )
f.   aggressive, grasping and conceited   (   )
g.   suspicious, cold and critical   (   )
h.   childish and given to seeking the limelight   (   )

AT TIMES I MAKE OTHER PEOPLE FEEL:

i.   superior and condescending towards me   (   )
j.   taken advantage of and angry with me   (   )
k.   unfairly treated and cold towards me   (   )
l.   impatient and indifferent towards me   (   )

Scoring

Add scores for each section as shown below   first horizontally and then vertically. Follow arrows.

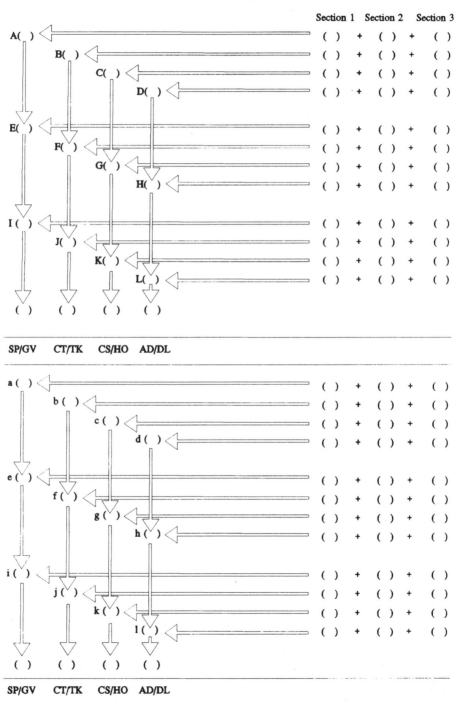

	Section 1		Section 2		Section 3
A( )	( )	+	( )	+	( )
B( )	( )	+	( )	+	( )
C( )	( )	+	( )	+	( )
D( )	( )	+	( )	+	( )
E( )	( )	+	( )	+	( )
F( )	( )	+	( )	+	( )
G( )	( )	+	( )	+	( )
H( )	( )	+	( )	+	( )
I ( )	( )	+	( )	+	( )
J( )	( )	+	( )	+	( )
K( )	( )	+	( )	+	( )
L( )	( )	+	( )	+	( )

( )   ( )   ( )   ( )

SP/GV   CT/TK   CS/HO   AD/DL

a ( )	( )	+	( )	+	( )
b ( )	( )	+	( )	+	( )
c ( )	( )	+	( )	+	( )
d ( )	( )	+	( )	+	( )
e ( )	( )	+	( )	+	( )
f ( )	( )	+	( )	+	( )
g ( )	( )	+	( )	+	( )
h ( )	( )	+	( )	+	( )
i ( )	( )	+	( )	+	( )
j ( )	( )	+	( )	+	( )
k ( )	( )	+	( )	+	( )
l ( )	( )	+	( )	+	( )

( )   ( )   ( )   ( )

SP/GV   CT/TK   CS/HO   AD/DL

Analysis

You can assess your resulting personal approach profile using the style descriptions below.

For example, a Supporting-Giving (SP/GV) bias indicates that you are thoughtful, somewhat idealistic and so on. *However*, if you score highly in SP/GV then you may be self-denying, impractical etc.

There are also indications of how to manage and influence people who have shown each particular bias in this test.

Personal style descriptions

	Productive use	Excessive use
Supporting– Giving style (SP/GV)	Thoughtful	Self-denying
	Idealistic	Impractical
	Modest	Self-denigrating
	Trusting	Gullible
	Helpful	Paternal
	Receptive	Passive
	Responsive	Over-committed
	Seeks excellence	Perfectionist
	Cooperative	Easily influenced
	Loyal	Obliged
Controlling– Taking style (CT/TK)	Controlling	Domineering
	Quick to act	Impulsive
	Self-confident	Arrogant
	Seeks change	Anarchistic
	Persuasive	Liable to distort
	Forceful	Coercive
	Competitive	Contentious
	Risk-taking	Gambling
	Persistent	Pressurising
	Urgent	Impatient

Conserving–Holding style (CS/HO)	Tenacious	Last-ditcher
	Practical	Uncreative
	Economical	Mean
	Reserved	Unfriendly
	Factual	Obsessed by
	Steadfast	statistics
	Thorough	Stubborn
	Methodical	Over-elaborate
	Detail-orientated	Plodding
	Analytical	Nit-picking
		Hypercritical
Adaptive–Dealing style (AD/DL)	Flexible	Inconsistent
	Experimenting	Aimless
	Youthful	Childlike
	Enthusiastic	Volatile
	Tactful	Avoids
	Adaptable	confrontation
	Socially skilful	Spineless
	Negotiating	Manipulative
	Animated	Over-compromising
	Inspiring	Melodramatic
		Self-deluding

Managing/influencing other people

	Supporting– Giving style	Controlling– Taking style	Conserving– Holding style	Adapting– Dealing style
How to influence a person according to each style	* Stress worthwhile causes * Idealistic appeals * Ask for their help * Show concern * Emphasize self-development	* Offer opportunity * Give more responsibility * Challenge * Provide resources to allow for achievement * Give authority	* Present ideas at low risk * Give opportunity to be analytical * Exercise logic, use facts * Use familiarity, routine and structure * Tie new things to old	* Change to do things with others * Use humorous appeals * Let them know you are pleased * Provide opportunities to be in the spotlight
Most effective environment for each style	* Respecting * Supportive * Reassuring * Idealistic	* Competitive * Direct * Risk-taking * Opportunistic	* Unemotional * Factual * Scientific * Practical	* Social * Changing * Youthful * Optimistic
Least effective environment for each style	* Betrayal * Personal criticism * Ridicule * Failure * Lack of support	* No resources * Authority countermanded * Responsibility diminished * No challenges * Can't control factors which affect results	* Constantly changing rules and policies * Highly emotional * Premature decision making * Failure to be taken seriously	* Unfriendly co-workers * Critical authority * Routine and details * Firm schedules and supervision
How to be the most effective boss for each style	* Give recognition, trust and appreciation * Mutual goal setting * Be accessible * Try to share * Be dependable	* Be confident * Provide autonomy * Reward results * Firm boundaries, but appreciate initiative * Listen, but be decisive * Spar on an equal basis	* Be organised * Show purpose * Detail-orientated * Systematic * Objective * Fair * Consistent	* Be friendly * Informative * Helpful feedback * Understanding * Encouraging * Flexible * Sense of humour
How to be the most effective employee to a boss of each style	* Demonstrate worth * Show loyalty * Be sincere * Team-orientated	* Be responsive * Capable * Independent * Direct	* Be respectful * Conforming * Logical * Pay attention	* Be sociable * Sophisticated * Tactful * Influential

8
Review

RELAX!

The interview is over and you have:

- got all the information you need;
- made the final sales pitch;
- invited objections – 'Have I assured you that I have the skills you need?'

Did you find out:

- what the level of responsibility is;
- how much authority you would have;
- what the prospects are;
- whether it is a successful organisation which attracts you;
- whether the job will satisfy your aspirations?

Have you enough information to decide whether a compromise on some of your requirements would be acceptable to you should an offer be forthcoming?

Now try to find a way of relaxing and taking your mind away from the interview.

Most of us feel we have performed reasonably well and come out feeling quite good (the adrenalin is still flowing) – except for those few occasions when we know we have 'blown it' completely.

Doubts tend to set in about 24 hours later – and increase from then on! We remember all the things we should have said and didn't, and the things we did say which we shouldn't have.

We convince ourselves that we have little hope, while at the same time hoping that everyone else was even more inane than we have convinced ourselves we were.

Of course, it's now too late to change anything so we must learn from our mistakes (if we made any) and look forward.

However, there is some action you can take. How keen are you to get this job? If it really means a lot to you, then why not take the trouble to write a short note to the interviewer (*no*, it will not be looked on as crawling!)

Dear Mr Byrd

Thank you for taking the time to see me yesterday and for your helpful response.

I would like to confirm my strong interest in the vacancy at your bank and, indeed, feel that I could make a definite contribution to your management team.

Should you want any further information, please do not hesitate to let me know. I hope to meet you again in the near future.

Yours sincerely

What does this achieve?

- It reaffirms your interest in the job.
- It reminds the interviewer of who you are 48 hours after the event.
- It is a courtesy that few interviewees offer.
- It cannot do any harm.

But do:

- make your letter short and to the point;
- make sure you get the interviewer's name and title right.

WHERE DO YOU GO FROM HERE?

The two major activities in any successful job search are:

- research – identifying opportunities;
- review – maintaining a structured approach to carrying out your job search plan.

The day following an interview, whether you know the result or not, is a good time to take stock of your situation – review your action plan – and ensure that you are going forward in the way which will produce the best results for you.

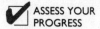 ASSESS YOUR
PROGRESS

Why not complete an interview assessment form? An example is given on page 112.

Having assessed your performance, make sure you are aware of your current situation by running through the following weekly checklist:

Weekly checklist

1. How many job applications are still outstanding?

2. How many job applications are still to be completed?

3. Are there any interviews arranged? When are they?

4. Are there any organisations I have identified but not yet contacted?

5. Have I checked the latest newspapers/magazines?

6. Have I contacted companies who have not replied?

7. Is it time to widen my search, either geographically or in the type/level of jobs I will consider?

8. Am I failing to get interviews despite the number of jobs I apply for?

9. Am I getting a good interview rate but no offers?

10. Am I keeping up my network contacts?

11. Are there other contacts I could be making?

12. Is there any other action I should be taking?

The record sheets on pages 112–115 may also be helpful.

Your checklist should form a regular part of your job hunting activity. It can highlight any weaknesses which may creep in without you realising they are there.

Suppose you are making lots of applications but not being invited to interviews. Perhaps:

- you are applying for unsuitable vacancies;
- your CV needs amending/better direction/shortening;
- your aspirations are too high in terms of position or salary or responsibility;
- you are pitching your applications too low – recipients feel you are over-qualified.

Getting interviews without offers of employment could mean:

- your interview technique needs reviewing;
- your CV is overstating your potential/expertise/skills;
- you aren't selling yourself in the face-to-face situation;
- your research/preparation/dress/presentation need reviewing.

Not identifying enough organisations could mean:

- you are too restrictive in your search;
- you must be more flexible in terms of salary/benefits/area;
- there are not many opportunities in your field/area and you must consider a change of direction either in jobs sought or locations;
- your research is not thorough enough to identify potential employers.

You must be prepared to analyse your progress on a regular basis and make adjustments to your action plan if you feel they are required.

If you identify problem areas but are not sure how to overcome them, seek advice from your family, contacts or ex-colleagues.

Interview assessment form

Date:
Organisation:
Job:
Interviewer:

Ground covered:
(Nature of the organisation/job; requirements; extent to which experience met requirements)

Particular points made about my areas of competence and experience in relation to the job:

Did I 'sell' my benefits (ie what I could bring to this organisation)?
If not, how can I improve?

Which questions did I find difficult to answer?

How could I improve on the way I presented myself?

Questions I should have raised (for future reference):

Next steps/actions I must take (who/when/what)

Record of job advertisements replied to

Date of application	Source and date of advert	Ref. no.	Job title	Company	Result	Notes and action to be taken

Direct approaches to potential employers

Organisation to contact and address	Person to contact and tel. no.	Date letter sent	Result	Comments and further action to be taken

Record of contacts with agencies

Agency contacted	Name, address and tel. no. of contact	Date of contact	Result	Date for follow-up	Notes and future action

9

Helping Yourself

CREATING OPPORTUNITIES FOR EMPLOYMENT

WHERE CAN YOU GET HELP?

MAKING THE MOST OF PAST EXPERIENCE

CREATING OPPORTUNITIES FOR EMPLOYMENT

Your research will often reveal companies that you would like to approach, feel you could help or who could use your expertise, but who will reject any approach for employment made to them because:

- they haven't identified their own need;
- they don't think they can afford any more staff;
- they haven't seen an opportunity to develop or grow that you have identified.

This is where your ingenuity and ability to sell your talents can make stonewalling into an opportunity.

BE IMAGINATIVE

Many companies, particularly smaller ones, will consider short-term, temporary or contract work as a solution to a problem or need. This is, of course, long-accepted practice in clerical or factory work. Companies like Brook Street and Manpower have built very successful, national businesses by fulfilling short-term requirements. Why shouldn't there be a similar market need in the professional, technical and managerial fields?

> The electronic and oil booms of the 1970s and 1980s created a shortage of good draughtsmen for both electronic circuitry and control systems incorporating electronics. The result was that those with the relevant skills and knowledge went out on short-term contracts at something like treble the normal hourly rate.
>
> The bubble burst in the recession of the late 1980s when many small firms went under and employment, rather than contract work, became the norm again. Much of this was due to the collapse of the growth of electronic warfare systems within the defence industry. Until the mid-1980s good electronic engineers, computer scientists, electronic draughtsmen and computer modellers who were prepared to work in the defence industry were at a premium.

Some areas have already been explored but most are, or have been regarded as, posts only suitable for long-term employment – without any good reason.

If you identify a need, why not offer your services on a temporary or part-time basis – as a temporary executive or 'texecutive'?

Many temporary posts have led to permanent positions once an employer is able to see the benefits brought by the new individual. Even if this does not happen, you are gaining work experience, improving your CV and making fresh and current contacts.

This kind of activity can often lead you down the road of self-employment, a route taken by many people made redundant in the big shake-out of the late 1980s and early 1990s. Becoming a 'consultant' or starting your own business can be a very gradual progression and can sometimes come about without an actual decision to go that way being taken. It is not a route for everyone – you must have definable expertise and be able to 'sell' the benefits you can bring to the people that matter. However, for some there is the satisfaction of 'filling their own in-tray' and creating their own levels of activity and income.

Once they have been involved in a successful period of running their own business, very few people want to return to employment. Of course there are problems, stresses and strains. Naturally there will be days when you wonder if you will have an income next month and why all those people who promised you work have suddenly become unavailable.

However, if you want to become your own boss a time of redundancy is probably a good time to begin.

WHERE CAN YOU GET HELP?

Enterprise Agencies

Wherever you live there will be an Enterprise Agency serving your area which can assist you with a vast range of problems:

- Are there any affordable premises in my area?
- Where can I get training in marketing?
- What is the EC legislation regarding widget exporting?
- Are there any other, local small businesses in my field?

Businesses registered with Enterprise Agencies usually stay on the register for a period of years and benefit from joint promotional activities and inter-business meetings.

The Agency will also be able to point you in the direction of further assistance, on either a local or national basis. This may be available to you through such organisations as:

- the Department of Trade and Industry;
- Chambers of Trade, Commerce or Industry;
- your local Training and Enterprise Council.

Department of Trade and Industry (DTI)

The DTI provides considerable assistance to small and medium-sized companies in terms of advice and guidance – sometimes funding is also available to help businesses move forward.

The DTI's consultants cover a range of expertise – including marketing, exporting and new product development – and often initial consultations are free of charge.

The Department's remit is governed by Parliament and is therefore subject to frequent modification as Government priorities change. It is best to consult the local office to find out what assistance is currently available.

Chambers of Trade, Commerce or Industry

The Chambers exist to further the aims of organisations within their catchment areas. Traditionally they were small organisations concerned with very local events – such as Christmas markets – but in the last decade many have grown and become very influential in lobbying Government and creating links with large and small concerns.

Some people feel that Chambers should become more akin to their German counterparts and take over responsibility from central Government for the delivery of training and business incentives in their areas through more direct links with the DTI.

Currently they are setting up 'one-stop shops' in some areas to provide information and services for small businesses.

Training and Enterprise Councils (TECs)

TECs are a fairly recent Government training initiative. They are *not* a branch of any Government department and are directed and controlled by local, prominent and interested business people.

Although funded by Government and required to carry out certain duties for the Department for Employment, such as training for unemployed young people (formerly the Youth Training Scheme), each TEC has considerable autonomy and flexibility within its own locality.

So how can a TEC help you?

Financial assistance
If you want to start your own business most TECs have programmes of financial assistance for business start-up for fairly short periods.

Similar to the now defunct Enterprise Allowance scheme, each TEC has its own variant. The duration and amount of financial support will be determined in consultation with one of the TEC's advisers and you will, of course, be required to show that you know what you are doing and have some prospect of success:

- You will need to have a business plan. A simple format is sufficient to demonstrate that you have researched your market and an example is shown on pages 121–126.
- You must show that you have sufficient funding to 'get the show on the road'.
- You must have the expertise to deliver the service or product that is the basis of your business.

What can you expect in return?

The amount of funding will depend on the assessment made by the TEC, but it could be, for example, £40 per week for a year up to £100 per week for six months.

Don't go to a TEC expecting a handout – they are in the business of backing winners.

Your Business Success – Finance Plan for start-up and new businesses

Whatever you do, keep these forecasts under review and make them a habit!

As with many parts of the business, you will no doubt have notes, calculations, assumptions on which the figures included in these forecasts are based. Store such information with the forecasts so that you, your accountant, your bank manager or any other interested party with whom you might discuss business finance in the future can refer to them.

Make these dynamic, working files – for your business success!

Profitability Forecast

Your profitability forecast will be a composite of your income and expenditure forecasts and will reflect all the major assumptions made for a specified duration, normally one year. The next step is to look at the financial implications of the conclusions you have reached and, in the light of your findings, predict how profitable your business is going to be.

It is essential that you have a good idea of whether or not your business is going to be profitable and whether you can take any action to make it more profitable. The emphasis here is on profit and not turnover.

Remember – turnover is vanity, profit is sanity!

Notes on completion

Show in each budget column your estimate of the amount of income and expenditure to be generated each month. If you are buying an existing business, it will be useful to refer to previous accounting results. VAT should be excluded from these figures if you are, or expect to be, VAT registered.

- *Sales* – estimate sales each month taking into account seasonal variations such as Christmas, bad weather, holiday periods, etc. You should analyse your sales by product groups as they may have different markets and therefore different sales patterns.
- *Other income* – show any other income expected, eg enterprise allowance payments, grants, etc.
- *Material/rent/rates etc* – show estimates of your expenditure bearing in mind that materials might have a direct relationship to sales. Items such as rent may be paid quarterly or half-yearly. However, the figures should be spread over the months involved. In this document you are concerned with when the income or expenditure is generated, not when it is paid.
- *Depreciation* – this is a percentage of your profits which must be put aside to allow you to replace assets when your current ones are worn out (typically this may be an amount equivalent to one-fifth of your machinery costs per year, ie 20 per cent).
- *Net profit/(loss)* – the difference between monthly income and expenditure. Where expenditure exceeds income (ie a loss), figures are usually shown in brackets.

Profitability Forecast (for months 1–6)

	Month: Budget	Actual	Month: Budget	Actual	Month: Budget	Actual	Month: Budget	Actual	Month: Budget	Actual	Month: Budget	Actual	Half-year totals Budget	Actual
Income														
Sales														
Capital														
Grants														
Total income														
Expenditure														
Materials														
Rent/rates														
Power, heat & light														
Insurance														
Telephone														
Travel/vehicle costs														
Postage/carriage														
Printing/stationery														
Advertising/publicity														
Marketing														
Accountancy/legal														
Wages/salaries														
Training/development														
Bank charges														
Bank interest														
Finance interest														
Depreciation														
General expenditure														
Total expenditure														
Net profit/(loss)														
Cumulative profit/(loss)														

Cashflow forecast

While a thorough knowledge of your business profitability is vital, it is even more important to know the state of the business cashflow. In other words, where your money is, where it is coming from and where it is going to. The cashflow forecast is the tool which will help you monitor your cash position.

Notes on completion
Show in each budget column your estimate of the money to be received or spent in each month. These figures should be directly related to your profitability forecast, eg sales created in January may generate payment in March.

Remember, however, that this forecast monitors cash movements and therefore the figures must include VAT – whether or not you are registered for VAT and whether or not you can reclaim VAT charged by your suppliers.

There are, however, some headings which vary slightly from the profitability forecast in their treatment:
- *Capital* – show here money introduced by partners or shareholders as capital.
- *Other receipts* – include grants etc here.
- *Bank charges* – commissions and other bank charges.
- *Rent/rates etc* – items paid quarterly etc should be shown when the payment is expected to be made.
- *Bank repayments* – of loans and interest.
- *Finance repayments* – payments to be made on hire purchase or other similar finance agreements.
- *Fixed asset purchases* – the buying of new/second hand assets (plant, machinery, tools, etc).
- *Net inflow/(outflow)* – the difference between the monthly inflows and outflows. Where the outflow exceeds the inflow (ie outflow of funds), figures are usually shown in brackets.
- *Cumulative inflow/(outflow)* – this is the addition of all net inflows and outflows up to and including the month concerned. If an opening bank balance is included, this will give the forecast closing balance or overdraft at the end of each month.

Cashflow Forecast (for months 1–6)

	Month: Budget	Actual	Month: Budget	Actual	Month: Budget	Actual	Month: Budget	Actual	Month: Budget	Actual	Month: Budget	Actual	Half-year totals Budget	Actual
Income														
Sales														
Capital														
Grants														
Total income														
Expenditure														
Materials														
VAT														
Rent/rates														
Power, heat & light														
Insurance														
Telephone														
Travel/vehicle costs														
Postage/carriage														
Printing/stationery														
Advertising/publicity														
Marketing														
Accountancy/legal														
Wages/salaries														
Training/development														
Bank charges														
Bank interest														
Finance interest														
Depreciation														
General expenditure														
Total expenditure														
Net inflow/(outflow) Cash balance at start of year														
Cumulative inflow/(outflow) year														

Details of profitability forecasts and cashflow forecasts have been extracted from the DTI publication *Your Business Success*, written and designed by the Durham Business Club and reproduced here with DTI permission.

A series of *Your Business Success* modules are available from the DTI to help you during the early years of your business activity.

Training

The TEC will also be able to show you how to get free training in a variety of topics essential to the new entrepreneur:

- bookkeeping;
- taxation;
- computers in business;
- marketing;
- market research;
- selling;

and many others. In Hampshire, for example, there is a range of 20 topics covering key business concerns. Each session takes one day, or two evenings, and is aimed at owner/managers of small businesses.

Career development

In addition to the help which they provide to businesses starting up, TECs should be seen as an essential port of call for any executive, professional or manager seeking to develop their career.

TECs are responsible for a range of services to the local community, often through contracted agencies, including training programmes, development of National Vocational Qualifications, local application of the Management Charter Initiative and help and guidance on career development. They will also have a good knowledge of the labour market within their designated area.

For example, in the north-west LAWTEC offers the following Key Technology Training courses:

- MA Export Marketing;
- MSc Business Administration (Information Technology);
- MSc Waste Management;
- MSc Digital Signal Processing Applications;
- Postgraduate Diploma in Audio-Video Electronic Systems Design;
- Postgraduate Diploma in Electronics and Systems for the Built Environment;
- Postgraduate Diploma in Fire Safety and Risk Management;
- HND Material Processing Technology;
- HND Project Engineering/Management and Quality Assurance;
- HND/C Mechatronics;
- HND/C Quality Management;
- HNC Management of Biotechnology;
- HNC Food Development and Production;
- HNC Mechanical Engineering;
- Hotel, Catering and Industry Management Association Professional Diploma;
- Postgraduate Diploma in Tourism, Leisure and Service Management.

These training opportunities could present you with an alternative to immediate employment. Applications are not restricted to those living in the areas covered by the TEC concerned.

The length of such courses ranges from a few weeks to a full academic year and the training provided is at university standard. Allowances may be paid for those who are eligible together with certain travel expenses.

Your local TEC may also be able to offer you financial support to obtain advice on career development. From December 1993 several TECS are taking part in a pilot programme to give vouchers to those in employment who wish to obtain help and advice on the best career path for them as individuals. For example:

- Do I need a vocational qualification?
- If so, which one is appropriate?
- What are the entry requirements?

● Could I obtain some form of accreditation towards a qualification as a result of my experience?

All these aspects, together with advice on changing direction, use of a computerised assessment and/or psychometric assessment, are available from recognised career consultants.

TECs are offering vouchers for around 50 per cent of the consultancy fees, redeemable by the consultants against services provided (the actual percentage will vary according to the service and the consultant's normal fees). TECs will maintain a register of consultants appointed by them as suitable to offer the discounted service in their area.

In addition employers may be eligible for similar assistance to help them develop their employees by means of career counselling and advice.

Your local TEC will have full details of the situation in your area.

Short-term placements

Among the other opportunities provided by the TECs are usually programmes for placing executives or professionals with companies for short periods of time to complete projects or assignments which will be of benefit to both the company and the individual. Similar programmes were operated by the former Manpower Services Commission under the title of the Management Extension Programme.

For example, the Sussex TEC offers an Access Executive Skills programme in the Brighton, Hove and Portslade area to companies with particular short-term needs.

The 'employing' organisation, having identified its need (for example the introduction of a new computer network), is supplied with details of people who are currently unemployed and who have the qualifications and experience to carry out the tasks. The organisation carries out interviews and selects an individual and then comes to a financial arrangement to recompense them for the work to be done. Normally the work should be able to be completed within six to twelve weeks.

It is amazing how often people contracted on a short-term basis become such an asset that the organisation decides to retain them.

TECs are able to devise programmes to suit their own areas and it is advisable to consult your local TEC to find out what is on offer. The address and telephone number of your nearest TEC will be found in the telephone directory.

MAKING THE MOST OF PAST EXPERIENCE

Most people in, or about to enter, the jobs market are aware of the value of professional or vocational qualifications.

Some professional qualifications are mysteries to those outside the profession to which they apply but essential if you wish to progress within the relevant field. For example, membership of the Institute of Marketing is a very useful qualification if marketing is your chosen profession. Similarly, becoming a Chartered Accountant is essential to reach the top of that area of expertise.

Many of these qualifications can only be obtained following long periods of study, either full or part time, and then passing the necessary examinations of the professional body concerned.

Over the last few years there have been many developments in the area of vocational qualifications following the formation of the National Council for Vocational Qualifications (NCVQ).

Negotiations have been taking place with professional organisations and bodies representing employers to find ways in which people can demonstrate 'accredited areas of competence' which relate to specific tasks. This accreditation need not represent a full qualification but could form a credit towards one.

There are also ways in which past experience and achievements, which can be proven and measured, can be accredited. Known as 'accreditation of prior learning' (APL), this process is potentially of great value to job seekers who do not hold normally recognised qualifications.

DON'T LOSE
OUT

Once again, the TECs are at the forefront of developments in this area and can normally point you in the direction of those who can help and advise on APL.

After redundancy there is a danger that the opportunity to secure irrefutable evidence of past learning may be lost unless the appropriate action is taken before the previous employer disappears. Early discussions with your local TEC are strongly advised if you feel this is an avenue you could usefully follow.

10
The Way Ahead

We said right at the start that finding a job is a job in itself.

In fact it is a full-time and very demanding job if you want to be successful.

You are now well along the road to becoming organised for your job search:

- You have done your self-analysis and compiled your core information.
- You have revised your CV and the basic document is now always available.
- You have decided on the kinds of post you want to apply for and the areas of work which attract you.
- You have identified some local employers who might need your skills.
- You have considered different ways of approaching various opportunities.
- You have looked at interview research skills and examined your own techniques.
- You will appraise the results of all you attempt and learn from them.
- You can see the benefits of a properly structured approach to the whole task of looking for a job and will continue to follow your plan.

In addition to all you do yourself, you must make full use of the other facilities available.

Keep in touch with your Jobcentre/Claimant Adviser so that you know what is on offer to help you, such as:

- job search seminars;
- restart courses;
- job review workshops;
- job clubs;
- resource facilities;
- TEC training programmes.

Visit the other agencies to see if they can help you:

- employment agencies;
- Enterprise Agencies;

- colleges;
- local authority centres and programmes;
- Chambers of Commerce.

Make full use of your local facilities, such as the reference library.

Keep in touch with people you have met on any courses, with the Employment Service advisers, with companies who have been sympathetic towards your approaches, with your agency contacts.

While there is a lot of help available, at the end of the day *you* are the one who will decide the way ahead. Only *you* can put the required amount of effort into your job search programme.

You will decide whether to keep going when things are disappointing and the future seems uninviting, when all your intensive efforts have come to nothing and when it is easier to give up.

Make sure that you maintain all your records and keep them in order. Don't let a day go by without reviewing where you are with your current efforts and checking whether you should be taking any more action.

By reaching the end of this book you have demonstrated your determination to succeed. Good luck!